WORLD
HISTORY SERIES ▪▪▪

The Internment of the Japanese

Titles in the World History Series

The Abolition of Slavery
The Age of Augustus
The Age of Exploration
The Age of Feudalism
The Age of Napoleon
The Age of Pericles
The Alamo
America in the 1960s
The American Revolution
Ancient America
Ancient Chinese Dynasties
Ancient Greece
The Ancient Near East
The Assyrian Empire
The Battle of the
    Little Bighorn
The Black Death
The Byzantine Empire
Building the Transcontinental Railroad
Caesar's Conquest of Gaul
The California Gold Rush
The Chinese Cultural Revolution
The Civil Rights Movement
The Cold War
The Collapse of the
    Roman Republic
Colonial America
The Computer Revolution
The Conquest of Mexico
The Constitution and the Founding of
    America
The Crimean War
The Cuban Missile Crisis
The Early Middle Ages
Egypt of the Pharaohs
The Enlightenment
The Great Depression
Greek and Roman Mythology
Greek and Roman Science

Greek and Roman Sport
Greek and Roman Theater
The History of Medicine
The History of Rock & Roll
The History of Slavery
The Incan Empire
The Internment of the Japanese
The Italian Renaissance
The Late Middle Ages
The Making of the Atom Bomb
Mayan Civilization
The Mexican-American War
The Mexican Revolution
The Mexican War of
    Independence
The Mongol Empire
The Persian Empire
Prohibition
The Punic Wars
The Reagan Years
The Reformation
The Renaissance
The Rise and Fall of the
    Soviet Union
The Roaring Twenties
Roosevelt and the
    New Deal
Russia of the Tsars
The Salem Witch Trials
The Space Race
The Spanish-American War
The Stone Age
The Titanic
Traditional Africa
Twentieth-Century Science
Viking Conquests
The War of 1812
World War II in the Pacific

WORLD
HISTORY SERIES

The Internment of the Japanese

by
Diane Yancey

LUCENT BOOKS
SAN DIEGO, CALIFORNIA

THOMSON

GALE

Detroit • New York • San Diego • San Francisco
Boston • New Haven, Conn. • Waterville, Maine
London • Munich

On cover: Soldiers escorting Japanese Americans to
Bainbridge Island evacuation camp.

Library of Congress Cataloging-in-Publication Data

Yancey, Diane.
    The Internment of the Japanese / by Diane Yancey.
        p.   cm.—(World history series)
    Includes bibliographical references and index.
    Summary: Discusses the relocation and internment of
Japanese Americans during World War II.
    ISBN 1-59018-013-5 (hardback : alk. paper)
    1. Japanese Americans—Evacuation and relocation,
1942–1945—Juvenile literature. 2. World War, 1939–1945—
Evacuation of civilians—Juvenile literature. 3. World War,
1939–1945—Concentration camps—United States—Juvenile
literature 4. World War, 1939–1945—Prisoners and prisons,
American—Juvenile literature. [1. Japanese Americans—
Evacuation and relocation, 1942–1945. 2. World War,
1939–1945—United States.] I. Title. II. Series.
D769.8 A6 Y359 2002
940.54 ' 7273—dc21

2001006270

Contents

Foreword

Each year on the first day of school, nearly every history teacher faces the task of explaining why his or her students should study history. One logical answer to this question is that exploring what happened in our past explains how the things we often take for granted— our customs, ideas, and institutions— came to be. As statesman and historian Winston Churchill put it, "Every nation or group of nations has its own tale to tell. Knowledge of the trials and struggles is necessary to all who would comprehend the problems, perils, challenges, and opportunities which confront us today." Thus, a study of history puts modern ideas and institutions in perspective. For example, though the founders of the United States were talented and creative thinkers, they clearly did not invent the concept of democracy. Instead, they adapted some democratic ideas that had originated in ancient Greece and with which the Romans, the British, and others had experimented. An exploration of these cultures, then, reveals their very real connection to us through institutions that continue to shape our daily lives.

Another reason often given for studying history is the idea that lessons exist in the past from which contemporary societies can benefit and learn. This idea, although controversial, has always been an intriguing one for historians. Those who agree that society can benefit from the past often quote philosopher George Santayana's famous statement, "Those who cannot remember the past are condemned to repeat it." Historians who subscribe to Santayana's philosophy believe that, for example, studying the events that led up to the major world wars or other significant historical events would allow society to chart a different and more favorable course in the future.

Just as difficult as convincing students of the importance of studying history is the search for useful and interesting supplementary materials that present historical events in a context that can be easily understood. The volumes in Lucent Books' World History Series attempt to present a broad, balanced, and penetrating view of the march of history. Ancient Egypt's important wars and rulers, for example, are presented against the rich and colorful backdrop of Egyptian religious, social, and cultural developments. The series engages the reader by enhancing historical events with these cultural contexts. For example, in *Ancient Greece*, the text covers the role of women in that society. Slavery is discussed in *The Roman Empire*, as well as how slaves earned their freedom. The numerous and varied aspects of everyday life in these and other societies are explored in each volume of the series. Additionally, the series covers the major political, cultural, and philosophical ideas as the torch of civilization is passed from ancient Mesopotamia and Egypt, through Greece, Rome, Medieval Europe, and other world cultures, to the modern day.

The material in the series is formatted in a thorough, precise, and organized manner. Each volume offers the reader a comprehensive and clearly written overview of an important historical event or period. The topic under discussion is placed in a broad, historical context. For example, *The Italian Renaissance* begins with a discussion of the High Middle Ages and the loss of central control that allowed certain Italian cities to develop artistically. The book ends by looking forward to the Reformation and interpreting the societal changes that grew out of the Renaissance. Thus, students are not only involved in an historical era, but also enveloped by the events leading up to that era and the events following it.

One important and unique feature in the World History Series is the primary and secondary source quotations that richly supplement each volume. These quotes are useful in a number of ways. First, they allow students access to sources they would not normally be exposed to because of the difficulty and obscurity of the original source. The quotations range from interesting anecdotes to farsighted cultural perspectives and are drawn from historical witnesses both past and present. Second, the quotes demonstrate how and where historians themselves derive their information on the past as they strive to reach a consensus on historical events. Lastly, all of the quotes are footnoted, familiarizing students with the citation process and allowing them to verify quotes and/or look up the original source if the quote piques their interest.

Finally, the books in the World History Series provide a detailed launching point for further research. Each book contains a bibliography specifically geared toward student research. A second, annotated bibliography introduces students to all the sources the author consulted when compiling the book. A chronology of important dates gives students an overview, at a glance, of the topic covered. Where applicable, a glossary of terms is included.

In short, the series is designed not only to acquaint readers with the basics of history, but also to make them aware that their lives are a part of an ongoing human saga. Perhaps then they will come to the same realization as famed historian Arnold Toynbee. In his monumental work, *A Study of History*, he wrote about becoming aware of history flowing through him in a mighty current, and of his own life "welling like a wave in the flow of this vast tide."

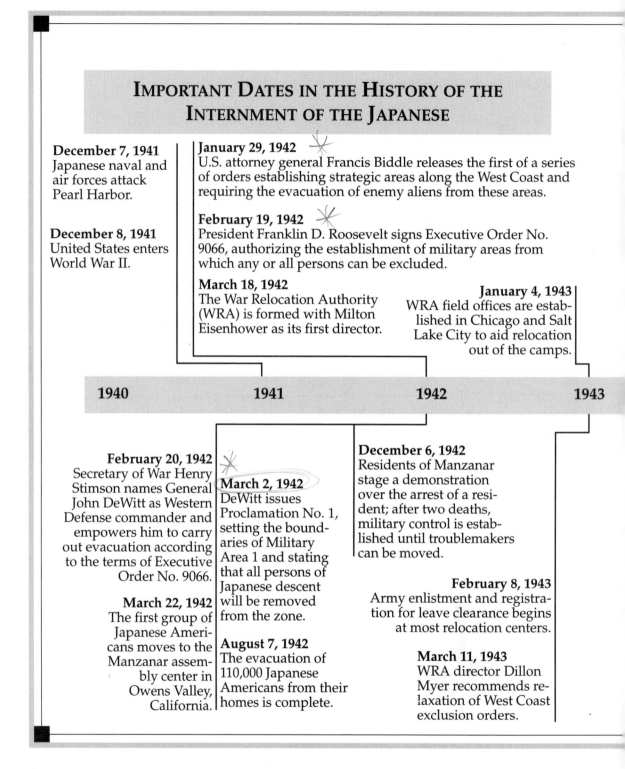

Important Dates in the History of the Internment of the Japanese

December 7, 1941
Japanese naval and air forces attack Pearl Harbor.

December 8, 1941
United States enters World War II.

January 29, 1942
U.S. attorney general Francis Biddle releases the first of a series of orders establishing strategic areas along the West Coast and requiring the evacuation of enemy aliens from these areas.

February 19, 1942
President Franklin D. Roosevelt signs Executive Order No. 9066, authorizing the establishment of military areas from which any or all persons can be excluded.

March 18, 1942
The War Relocation Authority (WRA) is formed with Milton Eisenhower as its first director.

January 4, 1943
WRA field offices are established in Chicago and Salt Lake City to aid relocation out of the camps.

1940   **1941**   **1942**   **1943**

February 20, 1942
Secretary of War Henry Stimson names General John DeWitt as Western Defense commander and empowers him to carry out evacuation according to the terms of Executive Order No. 9066.

March 22, 1942
The first group of Japanese Americans moves to the Manzanar assembly center in Owens Valley, California.

March 2, 1942
DeWitt issues Proclamation No. 1, setting the boundaries of Military Area 1 and stating that all persons of Japanese descent will be removed from the zone.

August 7, 1942
The evacuation of 110,000 Japanese Americans from their homes is complete.

December 6, 1942
Residents of Manzanar stage a demonstration over the arrest of a resident; after two deaths, military control is established until troublemakers can be moved.

February 8, 1943
Army enlistment and registration for leave clearance begins at most relocation centers.

March 11, 1943
WRA director Dillon Myer recommends relaxation of West Coast exclusion orders.

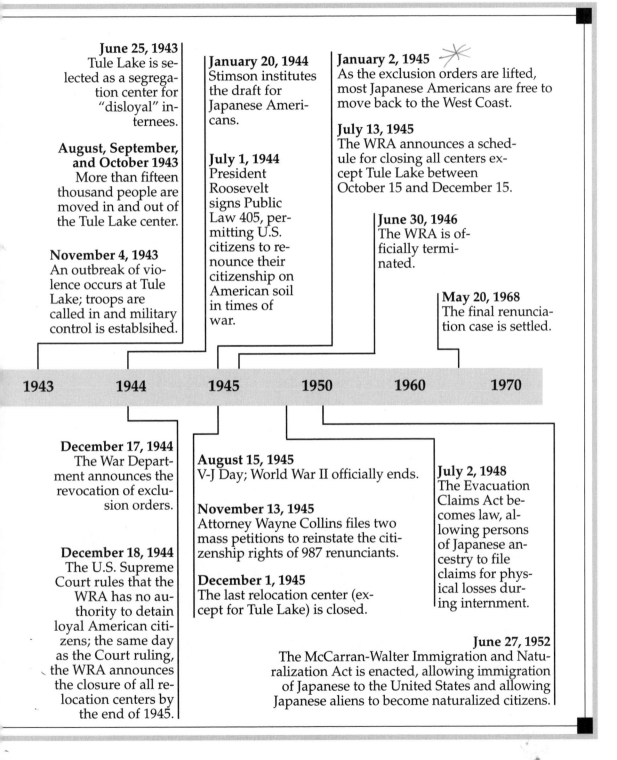

June 25, 1943
Tule Lake is selected as a segregation center for "disloyal" internees.

August, September, and October 1943
More than fifteen thousand people are moved in and out of the Tule Lake center.

November 4, 1943
An outbreak of violence occurs at Tule Lake; troops are called in and military control is establsihed.

January 20, 1944
Stimson institutes the draft for Japanese Americans.

July 1, 1944
President Roosevelt signs Public Law 405, permitting U.S. citizens to renounce their citizenship on American soil in times of war.

January 2, 1945
As the exclusion orders are lifted, most Japanese Americans are free to move back to the West Coast.

July 13, 1945
The WRA announces a schedule for closing all centers except Tule Lake between October 15 and December 15.

June 30, 1946
The WRA is officially terminated.

May 20, 1968
The final renunciation case is settled.

1943	1944	1945	1950	1960	1970

December 17, 1944
The War Department announces the revocation of exclusion orders.

December 18, 1944
The U.S. Supreme Court rules that the WRA has no authority to detain loyal American citizens; the same day as the Court ruling, the WRA announces the closure of all relocation centers by the end of 1945.

August 15, 1945
V-J Day; World War II officially ends.

November 13, 1945
Attorney Wayne Collins files two mass petitions to reinstate the citizenship rights of 987 renunciants.

December 1, 1945
The last relocation center (except for Tule Lake) is closed.

July 2, 1948
The Evacuation Claims Act becomes law, allowing persons of Japanese ancestry to file claims for physical losses during internment.

June 27, 1952
The McCarran-Walter Immigration and Naturalization Act is enacted, allowing immigration of Japanese to the United States and allowing Japanese aliens to become naturalized citizens.

Americans Betrayed

The camps were sprawling, tar-paper communities, made to hold thousands of men, women, and children. They were ringed with barbed wire and fitted out with watchtowers and gun-toting military guards. Authorities called them "relocation centers." Those who objected to the fact that the occupants were neither criminals nor prisoners of war, but simply members of a minority race, gave them an uglier name—concentration camps.

They were not located in Germany or Poland, they had not been authorized by Adolf Hitler's henchmen, and their in-

The Manzanar Relocation Center in California imprisoned thousands of American citizens and legal immigrants during World War II solely because they were of Japanese ancestry.

mates were neither Jews, Poles, nor Gypsies. These were American prisons, and they held persons of Japanese ancestry, at least half of whom were American citizens. Historian Roger Daniels writes, "It was the first and so far the only time that the American government has violated, en masse, the rights of an ethnic group, the second- and third-generation Japanese Americans, to which its Constitution had given citizenship."[1]

MILITARY NECESSITY

The decision to imprison Japanese Americans (a term used for all Japanese living in America) was a popular one in 1942. It was supported not only by the government, but it was also called for by the press and the people. In the wake of the bombing of Pearl Harbor, Hawaii, on December 7, 1941, Japan was the enemy. Many Americans believed that all persons of Japanese ancestry were potential spies and saboteurs, intent on helping their mother country win World War II. "The Japanese race is an enemy race," General John DeWitt, head of the Western Defense Command wrote in February 1942. "And while many second and third generation Japanese born in the United States soil, possessed of United States citizenship, have become 'Americanized,' the racial strains are undiluted."[2]

Executive Order No. 9066—which sent the Japanese to the camps—was signed in early 1942 by Franklin Delano Roosevelt, a president well known for his wisdom, benevolence, and defense of freedom. The

Supreme Court itself upheld the order because of "military necessity." "There was evidence of disloyalty on the part of some [Japanese Americans], the military authorities considered that the need for action was great, and time was short. We cannot—by availing ourselves of the calm perspective of hindsight—now say that at that time these actions were unjustified,"[3] stated Justice Hugo Black on December 18, 1944.

Within weeks of the order being signed into law, more than one hundred thousand Japanese Americans were evacuated from the West Coast and were put first into temporary assembly centers and then into more permanent relocation camps. For more than three years, they ate, slept, worked, and waited in these camps, hoping to demonstrate their patriotism by their cooperation. Daniels observes, "For the vast majority . . . loyalty was demonstrated by submissiveness to authority. The government said go, and they went, cooperating, organizing, submitting."[4] Only when the war was almost over—and a legal challenge to internment seemed likely to be upheld in the courts—were the camp gates opened and the residents allowed to return to their homes. By then, some were so demoralized by their experience that they found it difficult to take on the challenges of ordinary life again.

A NATIONAL CALAMITY

The internment of the Japanese stands as an example of what happens in a democracy when racism is unchecked and mass

Many Americans believed that all persons of Japanese ancestry were potential spies and saboteurs, intent on helping Japan.

hysteria replaces calm and rational thinking. Despite its significance, however, for many decades it was an overlooked episode in the nation's past. Those who had supported it felt it was an embarrassing mistake that was better forgotten. Its victims were too ashamed to speak. One writer states, "This was not one of the prouder moments in our collective past, and those who were victimized by that experience would not, and in many ways could not, even much later, publicly talk about their years as prisoners of their own government."[5]

Today, all that has changed. The episode is well known and discussed, from its racist beginnings to its long-delayed conclusion in 1985. The courage of the few who dared at the time to call it unconstitutional and inhumane has been noted and approved. The unconquerable spirit of the internees who turned the tragedy into triumph has been commended and celebrated.

Nevertheless, those who did not live through the experience are still inclined to wonder how America let it happen, why the internees marched so willingly off to camp, and why so many of them were unwilling to leave in the end. The answers—fascinating, bewildering, and horrifying—are part of a national calamity, the story of Japanese American internment.

1 The Japanese "Problem"

Anti-Asian prejudice was nothing new in America in the 1940s. Discrimination against Asians had occurred on the West Coast since the Chinese arrived in the 1850s. One historian explains it this way: "Anti-Japanese prejudice was in part an expression of American frontier behavior. In a western setting in which intolerance, vigilantism, and raw economic competition were the rule, the Asiatic immigrants, along with dudes, crooks, and fallen women, played the unwelcome roles of 'strangers in town.'"[6]

"Asiatic Hordes"

The Chinese who arrived at about the time of the Civil War were the first Asians to settle on the Pacific Coast of the United States. These immigrants were men who found jobs in mines and in railroad construction and were content to work long hours for low pay. By 1870 over sixty thousand Chinese in the United States made up about 10 percent of the population of California.

Many Caucasian workmen resented competing with these alien workers, whom they considered inferior because of their race. Laws were passed that denied Chinese immigrants their rights in such areas as employment and police protection. One historian writes, "There was a special tax on Chinese miners . . . and licenses to do business were often denied. Agitators portrayed the Chinese as Asi-

In the nineteenth century, Chinese workers were the first Asians to experience racism in America. Caucasian workers resented competing with the Chinese.

atic hordes bent upon overtaking and destroying the white populace."[7] Chinese immigrants were robbed, assaulted, and sometimes murdered by hostile whites.

In 1882, to limit the influx of Chinese into the United States, powerful trade unions worked to pass legislation that banned Chinese immigration. The Chinese Exclusion Act read, in part,

> Be it enacted by the Senate and House of Representatives of the United States of America in Congress assembled, That from and after the expiration of ninety days next after the passage of this act, and until the expiration of ten years next after the passage of this act, the coming of Chinese laborers to the United States be . . . suspended; and during such suspension it shall not be lawful for any Chinese laborer to come, or, having so come after the expiration of said ninety days, to remain within the United States.[8]

In the meantime, Japanese immigration had begun. Anti-Asian sentiment, once aimed just at the Chinese, would soon expand and be directed at the newcomers as well.

THE ARRIVAL OF THE ISSEI

Deprived of cheap Chinese labor, Westerners at first welcomed the arrival of Japanese laborers beginning in about 1890. Most of them were young men who were looking for freedom and a better life; many expected to return to Japan after making their fortunes. They worked on the railroads and in sugar-beet fields, fruit orchards, vineyards, and berry fields. Although their loyalty was to their homeland, they admired America as well and soon recognized its advantages. "As they lived long in this country, they found out it is a good place to live and their descendants have so much more opportunity,"[9] stated one immigrant.

Those immigrants who stayed were called Issei, or the first-generation Japanese in America. They began their new lives in poverty, but through a combination of hard work, honesty, and frugality, they improved their situation. From railroad construction and migrant labor they went on to establish small businesses such as laundries and restaurants. Union rules kept them out of manufacturing and construction, but commercial fishing was an option. Some purchased their own boats. A large number leased land and became truck farmers—that is, farmers who grow produce to be taken directly to market. As such, they often raised vegetables, fruits, and flowers that Caucasian farmers did not grow.

Japanese truck farmers sometimes worked against almost insurmountable odds. With little money for farm equipment, they cultivated their land almost by hand, enduring hours of backbreaking labor to plant, tend, and harvest crops. They often worked land that no one else wanted, turning deserts, swamps, and rocky ground into productive fields. Historian Masakazu Iwata states,

> They pioneered the rice industry, and planted the first citrus orchards in the hog wallow lands in the San Joaquin

Japanese truck farmers were instrumental in making California one of the greatest farming states in America.

Valley. They played a vital part in establishing the present system of marketing fruits and vegetables, especially in Los Angeles County. . . . From the perspective of history, it is evident that the contributions of the Issei . . . were undeniably a significant factor in making California one of the greatest farming states in the nation.[10]

Self-reliance was another motto of the Issei. Even during the Great Depression of the 1930s, when businesses failed and work was hard to find, few Japanese Americans went on welfare roles. Instead, when the lean times struck, they tightened their belts and, if necessary, turned to friends or family for help. "The Issei farmers were a self-sustaining people. I remember when supper was made from everything that grew on the farm,"[11] one man remarked.

EXCLUSION EFFORTS

As they became more established and successful, Japanese immigrants roused similar anti-Asian feelings that had been expressed when Chinese workers began competing with whites. Even at their peak in about 1930, they numbered less than 140,000 and made up only about 2 percent of California's population, but whites saw them as "flooding" the West Coast and resented it.

In 1900 San Francisco mayor James Duval Phelan was one of the first to speak out publicly. "The Japanese are starting the same tide of immigration which we thought we had checked twenty years ago. . . . Personally we have nothing against the Japanese, but as they will not assimilate with us and their social life is different from ours, let them keep a respectful distance."[12]

Efforts to limit their rights soon followed. The Asiatic Exclusion League was established in San Francisco in 1905, made up of dozens of businessmen who wanted Japanese immigration stopped. By 1908 the league had over one hundred thousand members and over two hundred affiliated groups, many of which were labor unions. League efforts included working to keep Asians out of labor unions, to segregate them from public schools, to bar them from American citizenship, and to prohibit them from owning land. In 1919 the Oriental Exclusion League formed, made up of numerous organizations including the California Federation of Labor, the American Legion, the State Grange, and the Native Sons and Daughters of the Golden West. Their demands included ending Japanese immigration and denying citizenship rights to all Asians, even those born in America.

SENSATIONALISM IN THE PRESS

"Yellow press" newspapers added to anti-Japanese sentiment on the West Coast. These papers often carried sensational and inflammatory articles about the "Japanese problem" and the "yellow peril." Many were owned by publishing mogul William Randolph Hearst. In 1905 even the conservative San Francisco *Chronicle* ran a series

WHITE CALIFORNIA

Only a few journalists, politicians, and businessmen were outspoken in their demands to exclude the Japanese from America in the 1900s, but a surprising number of ordinary people on the West Coast were anti-Japanese. Historian Roger Daniels discusses the strength of the movement in Concentration Camps, U.S.A.: Japanese Americans and World War II.

"How representative of white California were the exclusionists? The best possible measure of the popularity of the anti-Japanese position came in 1920, when a stronger Alien Land Act, one that prohibited leasing and sharecropping as well as land purchase, was put on the California ballot as an initiative. It passed by a margin of more than 3 to 1. Few of the more than six hundred thousand California citizens who voted for the measure can have been in any way actual or potential competitors with Japanese farmers; the measure carried every county in the state, and did well in both urban and rural areas. The simple fact of the matter was that Californians had come to hate and fear Japanese with a special intensity."

In 1923 homeowners and members of the Hollywood Association started a campaign to expel all Japanese families from the neighborhood.

titled, "The Japanese Invasion: The Problem of the Hour," and claimed that thousands of "little brown men" in the country were Japanese spies. Other *Chronicle* headlines of that period included "Brown Artisans Steal Brains of Whites" and "Japanese: A Menace to American Women."

Influenced by such sensationalism and pressured by labor groups, Western legislators responded predictably. They stated in 1905, "Japanese laborers, by reason of race habits, mode of living, disposition and general characteristics, are undesirable. . . . They contribute nothing to the growth of the state. They add nothing to its wealth, and they are a blight on the prosperity of it, and a great and impending danger to its welfare."[13]

From that year until about 1940, at least one anti-Japanese bill came before the California legislature each year. In 1905 a resolution was sent to Congress asking it to limit Japanese immigration. In 1913 the Alien Land Law barred the Issei from purchasing land and acquiring leases for longer than three years in California. Sim-

ilar land laws were later passed in Arizona, Washington, and Oregon.

THE GENTLEMEN'S AGREEMENT

Although a variety of anti-Asian measures were brought before Western legislatures during the early 1900s, one that caused an international incident occurred in San Francisco in 1906. That year, the city's school board announced that all Asian children would be barred from public primary schools, sparking a sharp response from the Japanese government. According to an 1894 U.S.–Japanese treaty, nationals in each country were guaranteed certain residential rights and privileges that included educational opportunities. In Japan, feelings ran so high that anti-American riots occurred, and some newspapers called for a show of military strength.

Aware that Japan was a strong military power that had to be handled carefully, President Theodore Roosevelt stepped in to work out a compromise, the Gentlemen's

Agreement of 1907–1908. Under its terms, San Francisco repealed its decision regarding school segregation, and Japan agreed to restrict Japanese immigration into the United States. No further workers' passports were issued, and immigration was confined to "laborers who have already been in America and to the parents, wives and children of laborers already resident there."[14]

The Gentlemen's Agreement seemed a satisfactory solution to most Westerners for a time. Anti-Japanese activists soon discovered that it contained a loophole, however: It allowed Japanese wives and children to enter the country and join their husbands. It also allowed Issei bachelors to marry and bring their new brides—the so-called picture brides—to America. The agreement remained in force until 1924, when the National Exclusion Act halted all Japanese immigration into the United States.

Marriage by Proxy

The arrival of the picture brides between 1905 and 1920 marked a unique period in Japanese American history. When a

Most Japanese "picture brides" came into America through the immigration station at Angel Island, California, between 1905 and 1920. Their passports and immigration papers were carefully checked.

AN ALIEN RACE

Fear of a Japanese "invasion" plagued many Westerners, who wanted America to be a "white" nation. Japanese in America never made up more than 0.02 percent of the U.S. population, but in 1921 an informal committee of senators and representatives from twelve western states met in Washington, D.C., with the purpose of stopping Japanese immigration. Their words are included in Roger Daniels's Concentration Camps, U.S.A.: Japanese Americans and World War II.

"The process of invasion has been aptly termed 'peaceful penetration.' The invasion is by an alien people. They are a people unassimilable by marriage. They are a people who are a race unto themselves, and by virtue of that very fact ever will be a race and a nation unto themselves, it matters not what may be the land of their birth.

Economically we are not able to compete with them and maintain the American standard of living; racially we cannot assimilate them. Hence we must exclude them from our shores as settlers in our midst and prohibit them from owning land. Those already here will be protected in their right to the enjoyment of life, liberty, and legally acquired property. . . .

The alternative (to exclusion) is that the richest section of the United States will gradually come into the complete control of an alien race. . . . A careful study of the subject will convince anyone who will approach it with an open mind that the attitude of California, and other states . . . is not only justifiable but essential to the national welfare."

lonely Issei bachelor could not afford to travel back to Japan to find a wife, his parents in Japan would carefully choose a woman they felt would be suitable. Investigations and negotiations followed to ensure that the prospective mates were healthy, of the same social status, and morally and economically acceptable to everyone concerned. Then the couple would exchange pictures through the mail. If both were satisfied, a marriage by proxy would take place (someone would stand in for the groom during the ceremony). The new bride would shortly thereafter board a ship for America to join her husband.

Not surprisingly, couples were often startled or dismayed when they met each other face-to-face. Women were not as attractive. Men were older or shorter or more poverty-stricken. A few brides were so disillusioned that they sailed back to Japan immediately. Some got a divorce after a time. Usually, however, couples successfully adjusted to each other and worked side by side to make theirs a successful marriage. Marriage by proxy continued to be popular until the Japanese government stopped issuing passports to picture brides in about 1920.

Children were a logical consequence of these new marriages. Growing Japanese American families outraged racist Caucasians, however, who had believed that the Gentlemen's Agreement would reduce the numbers of Japanese in the United States, not swell them. Rumors spread that the birthrate for Japanese families was extremely high and that soon the Japanese would outnumber Caucasians. Later studies proved that the birthrate was comparable to other couples in similar social and economic circumstances, but such statistics were not available at the time to quiet public fears.

Children born to immigrant parents were known as Nisei (the first generation born in America), and they were automatically U.S. citizens. Now Issei farmers had another loophole they could use to get around discriminatory laws. Legis-

A group of schoolchildren in San Francisco, California, recite the pledge of allegiance to the flag. In 1940 Japanese American children were as "Americanized" as the rest of their classmates.

lation in most Western states made it illegal for the Issei to buy land for agricultural use, but their U.S.-citizen children could. Many Issei parents purchased land in a child's name, appointing themselves guardians while the child was a minor.

NISEI: THE SECOND GENERATION

From their birth, the Nisei occupied a slightly more privileged position than their parents because of their citizenship. (Many Issei would have liked to become naturalized citizens, but U.S. laws prohibited the naturalization of Asians.) And, while the older generation accepted the fact that they would always be foreigners, the Nisei were resolutely American. They attended public schools, where they learned the lessons of democracy, freedom, and equality. They dressed like other American children in blue jeans and bobby socks. Although they were expected to speak Japanese at home and were taught Japanese values, English was their first language. Exceptions were the Kibei, young Japanese Americans who received an education in Japan. They were more like the Issei—more loyal to Japan and less comfortable in white society.

The Nisei were so Americanized that they often found their parents' customs embarrassing. One Nisei girl remembered, "I would cringe when I was with [my mother] as she met a Japanese friend on the street and began a series of bows, speaking all the while in Japanese."[15]

Many Nisei balked at going to Japanese language school in the afternoons and refused to conduct themselves with proper Japanese modesty. "Why do you take such big steps?" a mother scolded when her daughter refused to imitate the tiny steps of a proper Japanese woman. "You walk like a boy! Can't you be more feminine?"[16]

EXCEPTIONAL AND ASHAMED

Although the Nisei wanted to be seen as good Americans, they were well aware that they were considered second-class citizens. Anti-Japanese laws set a standard for discrimination in all walks of life. They were denied admittance to theaters, public swimming pools, barbershops, and the like. They were ignored by waiters and store clerks. They were excluded from school functions.

Such discrimination angered many Nisei. Ironically, however, many others believed they were inferior and deserved the ill treatment they regularly suffered. "Society caused us to feel ashamed of something that should have made us feel proud," a Nisei later wrote. "Instead of directing anger at the society that excluded and diminished us . . . so low was our self-esteem that many of us Nisei tried to reject our own Japaneseness."[17]

Sensitive to the prejudice that surrounded them, most silently endured the slights and hoped that discrimination would go away. To spare their own feelings and those of others, they often stayed among themselves and limited their interaction with Caucasians. For this, whites accused them of clannishness and an unwillingness to blend into American society.

In an attempt to gain acceptance and convince others of their worth, the Nisei became overachievers in school and model citizens in the community. One Nisei remembers, "There was no ethnic group as straitlaced as the Japanese. . . .

When you talk about delinquency and other crime, for us there was nothing but traffic tickets."[18] Some Nisei became members of the Japanese American Citizens League (JACL), an organization the Issei viewed as radical but young Nisei saw as a public expression of their patriotism. Its creed stated,

I am proud that I am an American citizen of Japanese ancestry, for my

CAUGHT BETWEEN TWO AMERICAS

Although the Issei saw their children as true Americans, reality was somewhat different for the Nisei. In his book Issei and Nisei: The Internment Years, *internee chaplain Daisuke Kitagawa explains the tension and conflict the younger generation experienced in their duel roles as American citizens and as people of Japanese ancestry.*

"To the Issei, the Nisei was an incarnation of America that had broken through the barriers. . . . 'Flesh of his flesh, bone of his bone,' the Nisei was *his* beyond dispute, and yet he was an American, too. The Nisei was there already! The gulf had been bridged. The wall of the partition had begun to crumble. . . .

The Nisei, however, constituted a threat in the minds of that segment of American society which was imbued with racist ideology. All kinds of measures were devised to treat the Nisei as other than an American citizen. . . . These racists attempted to misconstrue the state laws so as to exclude him from the public school system and from such normal citizenship rights as owning property and to prevent him from choosing his area of residence. With or without the law, the employment opportunities for the Nisei were severely limited, so that for all practical purposes he was not much better off than the Issei. . . .

The Nisei thus found himself caught between the two Americas—the one of his parents' dream and the one in which he was to live. . . . The law declared him to be a citizen; he himself had no sense of belonging to any other country; and yet in practice American society treated him as an undesirable alien."

very background makes me appreciate more fully the wonderful advantages of this nation. . . . [America] has given me an education befitting kings. She has entrusted me with the responsibilities of the franchise [vote]. She has permitted me to build a home, to earn a livelihood, to worship, think, speak and act as I please—as a free man equal to every other man.[19]

The Nisei's determined declaration of loyalty and gratitude was sincere, but it rang false to Americans who could see only that they looked "foreign." Discrimination, suspicion, and hostility continued. Even Nisei who graduated with top honors from colleges and universities were denied jobs in their chosen fields. Young men and women who trained to be teachers, physicians, and the like ended up working at their parents' fruit stands. The Nisei often joked that "whenever you saw beautifully stacked apples in the grocery store you knew they had been arranged by a college-trained engineer."[20]

FRIENDS AND SUPPORTERS

Fortunately for Japanese Americans, not every Caucasian was racist. Some families bought land for Japanese friends. Many public schools welcomed Nisei children and treated them well. In many neighborhoods, Caucasian and Japanese families were close and had easy give-and-take relationships. One Nisei remembers, "The first of the vegetables would go to our neighbors, they in turn would bring their venison from their hunting trips and trout from their fishing trips. . . . The children would go Easter egg hunting together. Mother would exchange recipes."[21]

In some areas of the country—particularly cities like Seattle—businesspeople were more tolerant and discrimination was less common. "We never did think about race," one Nisei woman remembers, "I guess Seattle was more or less a melting pot. We all got on well together."[22]

Some Caucasians did more than establish personal relationships with Japanese. They protested injustice and worked to promote fair treatment for all Japanese Americans. Men like missionary/reformer Sidney Lewis Gulick wrote about Japanese American communities with the aim of increasing Caucasians' understanding and tolerance. The Los Angeles *Express* spoke out against the passage of the 1924 Immigration Act, and a group of New York businessmen and university leaders sent apologetic cablegrams to Japan. The United Mine Workers of Utah accepted Japanese miners into their memberships when other unions would not.

RISING TENSION

Discrimination did not dim the loyalty that the Nisei felt for America. They knew that it was not a perfect nation, but it was one of the best in the world. Even

Japan attacked the U. S. Pacific fleet at Pearl Harbor on December 7, 1941. The lives of Japanese Americans were changed forever.

the Issei were, for the most part, content. They still loved their homeland, but most planned to stay forever in their adopted land, which offered them more opportunities than they had had in Japan.

Relations between the United States and Japan were about to change for the worse, however. By the late 1930s all Americans felt the rising tension as a militant Japan threatened U.S. interests in the Far East. Then came the bombing of Pearl Harbor. World events were about to play a cruel trick on people of Japanese ancestry in the United States.

Chapter

2 Definite Menace

On December 7, 1941, at 8:00 A.M. Honolulu time, hundreds of Japanese planes bombed Pearl Harbor, Hawaii, home of the U.S. Pacific Fleet. The attack lasted over two hours. Eight American battleships and thirteen other naval vessels were sunk or severely damaged. Almost two hundred American aircraft were destroyed in the early morning attack. Three thousand military personnel were killed or wounded.

The bombing of Pearl Harbor shocked and horrified America. Few people had imagined that Japan would have the audacity to attack a world power like the United States. The event stunned Japanese Americans as much as everyone else. "The news hit us like a bomb," said one college student. "We never left the radio the rest of the day. We were really shocked."[23]

THE FACE OF THE ENEMY

Within a day, President Franklin D. Roosevelt asked Congress to declare war on Japan. Knowing that many Americans believed them to be loyal to the enemy, Japanese Americans worried. The Issei were not U.S. citizens and thus could rea-

sonably be called "enemy aliens." Many had their names on membership rosters of patriotic organizations that swore loyalty to Japan. Realizing that such details would weigh against them, they did what they could to improve their situation. They destroyed everything that might be judged suspicious or dangerous. Samurai swords, Japanese books and newspapers, Japanese flags, and even cherished family mementos were burned or buried.

The Nisei were uneasy but more confident. They were citizens and, theoretically at least, their rights would be protected. America was a land of liberty and justice. They would not be unjustly branded "the enemy" just because they had Japanese faces. They would be judged innocent until proven guilty.

To demonstrate their loyalty, however, some purchased war bonds, joined the Red Cross, volunteered for civilian defense patrols, and donated blood. Many young men decided to join the military even before they could be drafted. The leadership of the Japanese American Citizens League (JACL) sent a telegram to the president emphasizing their loyalty. The organization also urged all citizens to inform the government of any anti-American activity they discovered among their fellow Japanese. "As Americans we now function as counterespionage," editor Togo Tanaka stated on radio. "Any act or word prejudicial to the United States committed by any Japanese must be warned and reported to the F.B.I., Naval Intelligence, Sheriff's Office, and local police."[24]

FBI ROUNDUP

Concern in the Japanese American community was well founded, although at first it seemed that only the Issei would be affected. Because World War II was raging in Europe, American security agencies had already made plans to intern enemy German and Italian aliens if the United States entered the conflict. In mid-1940 Congress had passed the Alien Registration Act, which required all aliens over the age of fourteen to be registered and fingerprinted. The Department of Justice had put together a list of dangerous or subversive German, Italian, and Japanese individuals who could be arrested at a moment's notice if necessary.

Within hours after the Pearl Harbor attack, Federal Bureau of Investigation (FBI) agents began to take into custody three thousand aliens who, because of their associations, behavior, and/or ancestry, were potential enemies of the United States. About half of the three thousand were of German and Italian descent. The rest were Japanese.

The arrests were sudden and frightening, as one Nisei girl describes. "Two FBI men in fedora hats and trench coats—like out of a thirties movie—knocked on [my

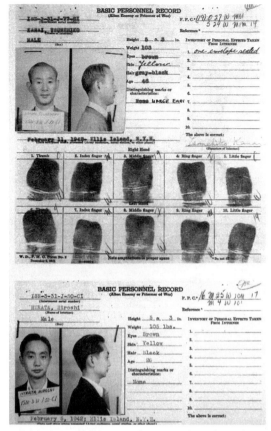

Within hours of the attack on Pearl Harbor, the Federal Bureau of Investigation arrested about fifteen hundred people of Japanese ancestry and imprisoned them for many months.

brother] Woody's door, and when they left, Papa was between them. He didn't struggle. There was no point to it. . . . He was suddenly a man with no rights who looked exactly like the enemy."[25]

Some Issei were arrested because they had money in Japanese banks, others because of their occupations or positions in the community. A number worked for Japanese import-export firms and had opportunities to bring weapons into the country. A number were commercial fishermen and could conceivably signal enemy ships off the coast. Some were community leaders, including ministers, Sunday school teachers, language teachers, and journalists. The FBI believed that it would be better to be safe than sorry when it came to deciding who might pose a threat.

All those arrested were taken to Justice Department internment camps located

SUBMARINES AND AIR RAIDS

After the bombing of Pearl Harbor, nervous Californians worried that a Japanese attack on the West Coast was about to take place. General John DeWitt played up those fears, and two incidents in February 1942 seemed to support his prediction that trouble was on the way. Authors Audrie Girdner and Anne Loftis explain in The Great Betrayal: The Evacuation of the Japanese-Americans During World War II.

"Confirming the fears of a nervous population, a Japanese submarine surfaced off the coast of Goleta near Santa Barbara on the evening of February 23 and began shelling an oil refinery. The fifteen-minute attack took place during a nationwide broadcast by President Roosevelt. No one was hurt and no fires were started. The end of a wooden jetty was splintered. Most of the twenty-five five-inch shells fired fell harmlessly into fields and canyons. But the attack, which seemed to many to presage [foreshadow] the long-predicted Japanese invasion, sent residents of the area into a panic. Tokyo boasted, 'This military feat has completely unnerved the entire Pacific Coast of the United States.'

[Then] out of the dark night sky came an 'air raid' on February 24 and 25 on Los Angeles which proved to be a false alarm. . . . The appearance of unidentified aircraft touched off a barrage of sirens and anti-aircraft fire. [A local newspaper reported,] 'Madness was loosed. The city was blacked out. Searchlights stroked the sky. Anti-aircraft guns opened up. The night was laced with tracers and explosions.' Falling ackack [debris] damaged houses and autos. Two people died of heart attacks and three were killed in traffic accidents in what was described as the worst transportation tieup in history. . . . According to the twenty-five-year commemorative report of the Los Angeles *Times*, 'Months later, it was concluded that the great air raid was set off by nothing more than one small, lost U.S. weather balloon.'"

throughout the United States. There they remained for many months while they were thoroughly investigated. Of all of the Japanese arrested at the time, only one, Tsutomo Obana, was found guilty of wrongdoing. Obana did business with the Japanese government and had neglected to register as a foreign agent. He was sentenced to a short term of prison for his misdeed.

THE RINGLE AND MUNSON REPORTS

After the initial round of arrests, the FBI considered that the greatest danger from fifth-column treachery (subversive acts carried out in a country by a disloyal population) was over. Their judgment was based on several reports filed by naval lieutenant commander Kenneth D. Ringle and State Department representative Curtis B. Munson in 1941. Ringle, who spoke Japanese, had been assigned to observe the Japanese community in southern California to determine its loyalty. His investigations ranged from befriending Japanese American individuals, who then served as informants, to reading secret documents that stated that Japanese diplomats mistrusted all Japanese Americans because of their loyalty to America. Ringle reported that "better than 90% of the Nisei and 75% of the original immigrants were completely loyal to the United States."[26]

Curtis Munson interviewed California businessmen, educators, religious leaders, and army and naval intelligence officers, including Ringle. He learned that few Japanese worked in manufacturing or industrial plants where they could spy or commit sabotage. He noted that their distinctive appearance would draw attention if they tried to carry out undercover work. He later wrote, "As interview after interview piled up, those bringing in results began to call it the same old tune. . . . There is no Japanese 'problem' on the Coast. There will be no armed uprising of Japanese."[27] Munson's and Ringle's reports were not publicized, however, so Americans had no chance to learn the truth about the Japanese American community.

FEAR, GREED, AND HATE

Anti-Japanese elements on the West Coast would not have been convinced by Munson's reports anyway. They were certain that all Japanese Americans were threats and ought to be locked up or sent back to Japan. Some who felt this way were motivated by fear. They had read newspaper statements by Secretary of the Navy Frank Knox, blaming the Pearl Harbor attack on fifth-column activity in Hawaii and were afraid a similar attack was planned for the West Coast. (In fact, no fifth-column activity by Japanese Americans was ever proven in Hawaii.)

Some groups were motivated by greed. For instance, the Grower-Shipper Vegetable Association admitted that Japanese farmers were competitors whom they wanted to remove. "We're charged with wanting to get rid of the Japs for selfish

Secretary of the Navy Frank Knox, (seated, right) *briefed the press, telling them he believed that an attack similar to Pearl Harbor would occur on the West Coast.*

reasons. We might as well be honest. We do. . . . If all the Japs were removed tomorrow, we'd never miss them in two weeks, because the white farmer can take over and produce everything the Jap grows. And we don't want them back when the war ends either."[28]

Some groups were motivated by racism. The most vocal were spokesmen for the yellow press who stirred up rumors and speculation with their emotional articles. Headlines screamed "Japanese Here Sent Vital Data to Tokyo" and "Two Japanese with Maps and Alien Literature Seized," although there was no truth in the articles that followed. Columnists and radio announcers emphasized that the West Coast was a "zone of danger" and made calls for vigilantes who could help the military get rid of Japanese spies, saboteurs, and fifth columnists. One columnist, Henry McLemore in the *San Francisco Examiner,* was particularly vicious in his opinions. "Herd 'em up, pack 'em off and give 'em the inside room in the badlands. Let 'em be pinched, hurt, hungry and dead up against it. . . . Let us have no patience with the enemy or with anyone whose veins carry his blood. . . . Personally, I hate the Japanese. And that goes for all of them."[29]

Articles made no distinction between Japanese and Japanese Americans, often referring to both as "mad dogs" and "yellow vermin." As one journalist for the *Los Angeles Times* wrote about the Nisei, "A viper is nonetheless a viper wherever the egg is hatched—so a Japanese American, born of Japanese parents—grows up to be a Japanese, not an American."[30]

Racist Leadership

Western politicians and civic leaders such as California congressman Leland Ford, California senator Hiram Johnson, and mayor of Los Angeles Fletcher Bowron also spoke heatedly against the Japanese American community at this time. Bowron stated, "Right here in our own city are those who may spring to action at an appointed time in accordance with a prearranged plan."[31] Representing other states, the mayor of Portland, Oregon, stated, "I believe . . . that the only reason the fifth columnists haven't struck so far is because their respective governments haven't given them the go-ahead."[32]

Such emotional and racist statements did much to influence the public, which had no way of knowing that most of what they heard and read was biased or false. As a result, public attitudes became more hostile. Japanese Americans lost jobs, received threatening phone calls, and were even physically attacked. Surveys carried out by the National Opinion Research Center in March 1942 showed that over 90 percent of those questioned supported relocating Japanese aliens off the West Coast and almost 60 percent favored the same treatment for citizens. Two-thirds of those polled believed Japanese Americans should be treated as prisoners of war.

The Army Bureaucrat

While the Justice Department was determining the loyalty of Japanese Americans on an individual basis, the War Department was disposed to take more drastic action. One of the most reactionary was General John DeWitt, head of the army's Western Defense Command, the department responsible for defending the West Coast. DeWitt was a sixty-one-year-old army administrator, a racist, and an alarmist. He was also convinced that Japanese Americans were a definite threat to the United States. He stated at a government conference on January 4, 1942,

> We are at war and this area . . . has been designated as a theater of operations. . . . (There are) approximately 288,000 enemy aliens . . . which we have to watch. . . . I have little confidence that the enemy aliens are law-abiding or loyal in any sense of the word. Some of them yes; many, no.

General John DeWitt, in charge of defending the West Coast, was convinced that Japanese Americans were a definite threat to the United States.

A Troublesome Problem

Although a mass evacuation of the Japanese off the West Coast was acceptable to many politicians, the idea of forcing Italians and Germans from their homes made them pause. Author Page Smith explains why in Democracy on Trial.

"One of the persistently troublesome issues had to do with the evacuation of Italian and German alien enemies. . . . The mayors of two of the nation's largest cities—San Francisco and New York—were Italian Americans. What of their parents? And, most troubling of all, what about Joe DiMaggio's father, a resident of Oakland, California, and thus subject to removal in any mass evacuation of the West Coast. The average American not of Italian ancestry might be indifferent to the fate of Mayor Angelo Rossi's parents or Mayor Fiorello La Guardia's, but if anything rude or uncivil were done to Joe DiMaggio's father, the popular reaction was bound to be highly unfavorable. To offend America's greatest hero since Babe Ruth would be impolitic [unwise] to say the least."

Baseball star Joe Dimaggio (right) *with his father.*

Particularly the Japanese. I have no confidence in their loyalty whatsoever. I am speaking now of the native born Japanese—117,000—and 42,000 in California alone.[33]

DeWitt used all of the rumors and false reports circulating in the press to support his position that all Japanese needed to be moved off the West Coast before they did serious damage to the war effort. In reporting to the Justice Department and others, he included instances of unidentified radio transmissions, mysterious signal lights, submarine attacks off the California coast, and discovery of hoards of weapons, radio receivers, and cameras. "I include all Germans, all Italians who are alien enemies and all Japanese who are native-born or foreign born," he stated. "I place the following priority. . . . First the Japanese . . . the most dangerous . . . the next group, the Germans . . . the third group, the Italians. . . . We've waited too long as it is. Get them all out."[34]

JUSTICE GIVES IN

Despite DeWitt's urgings, the Justice Department, represented by Attorney General Francis Biddle, maintained that the Japanese threat was not as serious as many thought. The enemy radio signals that DeWitt reported were in fact U.S. Army transmissions, signal lights were farmers burning brush in their fields, and rare submarine attacks never involved Japanese Americans. In the case of the weapons report, DeWitt had ignored the fact that most weapons had been seized from a licensed gun shop and a warehouse. In fact, there were no verified cases of shore-to-ship signaling, sabotage, or fifth-column activity by Japanese Americans on the West Coast during this period. The FBI and Justice Department later reported, "We have not found a single machine gun, nor have we found any gun in any circumstances indicating that it was to be used in a manner helpful to our enemies. We have not found a single camera which we have reason to believe was for use in espionage."[35]

Biddle was also concerned about the constitutionality of locking up innocent American citizens. Forcing the Nisei to leave their homes without justifiable rea-

In early 1942 Secretary of War Henry Stimson was swayed by General DeWitt's allegations.

sons raised serious legal questions. He said in December 1941, "If we care about democracy we must care about it as a reality for others as well as for ourselves; yes, for aliens, for Germans, for Italians, for Japanese . . . for the Bill of Rights protects not only American citizens, but all human beings who live on our American soil, under our American flag."[36]

Slowly, however, DeWitt's urgings and the insistence of anti-Japanese forces began to have their effect. On January 29 Biddle agreed to the establishment of exclusion zones around military installations, oil fields, dams, airports, and other sensitive areas. He agreed that Japanese, German, and Italian aliens would be evacuated from those areas.

On February 17, after Secretary of War Henry L. Stimson became convinced that

DeWitt's demands were justified, Biddle gave in to the inevitable. After lodging a final protest, and pointing out that moving one hundred thousand people raised very difficult questions of transportation and resettlement, he warned, "If complete confusion and lowering of morale is to be avoided, so large a job must be done after careful planning."[37]

FDR DECIDES

Although Biddle was reluctant, Stimson had little work to do to convince the president that action needed to be taken on the West Coast. Roosevelt was willing to believe the army and the War Department when they said that the removal of all Japanese—aliens and citizens—from the West Coast was a military necessity. On February 19, 1942, he signed Executive Order No. 9066, which officially authorized the evacuation of the Japanese American population. The order read, in part,

> By virtue of the authority vested in me as President of the United States, and Commander in Chief of the Army and Navy, I hereby authorize and direct the Secretary of War . . . to prescribe military areas in such places and of such extent as he . . . may determine, from which any or all persons may be excluded. . . . The Secretary of War is hereby authorized to provide for residents . . . such transportation, food, shelter, and other accommodations as may be necessary . . . to accomplish the purpose of this order.[38]

Some thought was given to rounding up and imprisoning all German and Italian aliens, but officials quickly realized that moving over 1 million people into detainment camps was not practical. Nor would it have been politically acceptable. Many Germans had fled to America to escape imprisonment or death in Hitler's Germany, and to detain them would have been cruel and traumatic. Thus, in general, only those German and Italian persons and their families who were classed as dangerous were excluded from militarily sensitive areas or placed in internment camps.

FOR THE GOOD OF THE COUNTRY

Roosevelt's decision to evacuate the Japanese met some opposition, but not as much as might have been expected. Most people accepted reports that evacuation was a necessary sacrifice for the good of the country. They believed that the army probably knew its business. Church leaders and academics protested the evacuation of a group based solely on race. The provost of the University of California stated that the order struck "an unprecedented blow at all our American principles."[39] At least one group of two hundred concerned citizens sent a letter to the president pointing out that prejudice and greed seemed to be motivating factors for the decision.

One of the most notable to speak out against evacuation was American Civil Liberties Union (ACLU) cofounder Norman Thomas, who sent a letter to President Roosevelt begging him to cancel the

Norman Thomas was the first to strongly and publicly voice opposition to the violation of the civil liberties of Japanese Americans.

order. Thomas was one of the first to state publicly that evacuation was a threat to America's democratic principles. In speeches, radio addresses, and written articles, he argued that the drastic handling of the Japanese "problem" in the West was much like "burning down Chicago to get rid of gangsters. . . . It will be taken in other countries as another proof of racial arrogance. The worst feature of the whole bad business is the small volume of protest and the considerable volume of applause . . . for this establishment of military despotism."[40]

Thomas stood practically alone, however, since the ACLU, created to fight the violation of American liberties, was divided over the issue of internment. Many who made up its leadership agreed that Executive Order No. 9066 was "unques-

tionably the most serious violation of civil rights since the war began,"[41] but they hesitated to take a strong stand against the president. Roosevelt was known as a champion of the underdog. It was difficult for them to believe that he would approve such a serious step without good reason.

Roosevelt would not have been swayed by the arguments anyway. Biddle later observed, "I do not think he was much concerned with the gravity or implications of his step. . . . What must be done to defend the country must be done. . . . Nor do I think that constitutional difficulty plagued him—the Constitution has never greatly bothered any wartime President."[42]

BETRAYED!

In early March 1942 General DeWitt announced the first steps in his evacuation plan: the formation of Military Area 1, which included the western half of Washington, Oregon, and California, and the southern half of Arizona. All persons of Japanese ancestry would be excluded from that area in the near future. Military Area 2 included the remainder of those four states and was unrestricted except for certain "prohibited zones." (In June, DeWitt included all of California in Military Area 1.) The exclusion orders applied to all full-blooded Japanese, aliens and citizens alike, and to anyone who had Japanese blood—no matter how small the quantum.

Among the Japanese American community, DeWitt's announcement was met with disbelief. The orders were seen as a betrayal and a violation of rights, particularly by the Nisei. They had been model citizens and had given the government no reason to believe that they would take part in sabotage or undercover activities. The injustice of the situation rankled. Saburo Kido, the president of the JACL, stated, "Never in the thousands of years of human history has a group of citizens been branded on so wholesale a scale as being treacherous to the land in which they live. We question the motives and patriotism of men and leaders who intentionally fan racial animosity and hatred."[43]

Veterans of World War I, such as Joe Kurihara, were especially outraged since they had already proven their loyalty by fighting for their country. "Having had absolute confidence in Democracy, I could not believe my very eyes. . . . America, the standard bearer of Democracy, had committed the most heinous crime in its history." And when Secretary of War Stimson made an attempt to justify Roosevelt's actions by citing not only military necessity but also concerns for the safety of the Japanese American community, many Nisei scoffed. "The government could have easily declared Martial Law to protect us,"[44] Kurihara pointed out.

Despite their outrage, few Japanese Americans actively resisted. Their traditions and upbringing led them to obey authority. Although some protested, signed petitions, and attended meetings, these groups were not well organized and had little power to resist a presidential decree. The JACL was even quick to express a willingness to cooperate. "We trust that the sacrifices which all of us may be called upon to make will create a greater and unified America when we have won the war,"[45] said Saburo Kido.

The Issei were even inclined to greet the official tidings with relief. They had been living in a state of uncertainty for weeks. Their bank accounts had been frozen because of their alien status, forcing them to live a hand-to-mouth existence. Many feared for their safety every time they left their homes. Others got tired of being harassed. "We can't step out of our homes to buy food without some hoodlum of a cop trying to run us in," one man said angrily. "I'll be glad to get out of this place! I hope I never see it again!"[46]

WHAT HAPPENS NEXT?

The evacuation of over one hundred thousand people was not a task to be taken lightly. Neither DeWitt nor anyone else had ever considered where such a large group of people could be moved, who would move them and how, what would be the cost of such a project, what evacuees would do with their property, and so forth. Stimson noted in his diary on February 27, 1942, "There was general confusion . . . arising from the fact that nobody realized how big it was, nobody wanted to take care of the evacuees, and the general weight and complication of the project."[47]

The confusion, and the contradictory orders that were given as a result of it, created nothing but trauma for Japanese Americans in the days ahead.

Chapter

3 Military Necessity

The army's first attempt at evacuation was called "voluntary," although there was really nothing voluntary about it. Japanese Americans were told that they had to be out of certain areas in a short period of time or face the consequences. The government avoided many of its decision-making problems, however, by leaving everything up to the evacuees. Not only did they have to find places to go, but they also had to decide how they would get there, and how to make a living when they arrived. They were also faced with disposal of their property and possessions in a short period of time.

Many of the first Japanese Americans to move opted to transfer the shortest distance possible, just outside the prohibited area. Others decided to strike out and resettle in neighboring states such as Nevada, Idaho, and Utah. To their dismay, they discovered that residents of these states were as prejudiced and as hostile as those at home. Banners across storefronts read, "Japs Keep Moving." Restaurants posted signs that said, "This restaurant poisons both rats and Japs."[48] Some groups were turned back at state lines. In Utah, a road crew threatened to stone one family

who was passing by. Encountering such unfriendliness, many families turned around and went back to the coast.

WAR RELOCATION AUTHORITY

By March, DeWitt realized that it was unrealistic to expect the Japanese to move rapidly out of Military Area 1 given the hostility they met at every turn. On March 27 he called a halt to voluntary evacuation. Families who had been told that they had to move now learned that they were prohibited from going anywhere at all until so directed by the army.

Next, since no Caucasians wanted Japanese living at large in their neighborhoods, DeWitt authorized the creation of temporary living accommodations. The War Relocation Authority (WRA) had already been established on March 18, 1942, and it was put in charge of evacuees once they were moved out of prohibited zones. Milton Eisenhower was the WRA's first director (replaced by Dillon S. Myer in June 1942).

The WRA's assignment was enormous: to supervise, find jobs for, and resettle almost one hundred thousand internees. Both Eisenhower and Myer soon discovered that the task that had been set before them was even more complex than they had imagined. They had to learn by trial and error the best way to manage relocation camps and their residents. "Neither I nor most of my staff were well informed regarding the problems we faced," Myer later stated. "We lacked information about the evacuees and their history. We were generally uninformed regarding the

---

TRAGEDY ON TERMINAL ISLAND

Some of the first Japanese Americans to be evacuated were a small colony of thirty-five hundred fishermen and their families who lived on Terminal Island in Los Angeles harbor, site of an airfield and two shipyards. Their story, recounted in the Commission on the Wartime Relocation and Internment of Civilians report, Personal Justice Denied, *provides a vivid impression of the hardship brought about by the evacuation.*

"On February 10, 1942, the Department of Justice posted a warning that all Japanese aliens had to leave the island by the following Monday. The next day, a Presidential order placed Terminal Island under the jurisdiction of the Navy. By the 15th, Secretary of the Navy Frank Knox had directed that the Terminal Island residents be notified that their dwellings would be condemned, effective in about 30 days. . . . [Then] on February 25 the Navy informed the Terminal Islanders that they had 48 hours to leave the island. Many were unprepared for such a precipitous move.

The FBI had previously removed individuals who were considered dangerous aliens. . . . As a consequence, the heads of many families were gone and mainly older women and minor children were left. With the new edict, these women and children, who were unaccustomed to handling business transactions, were forced to make quick financial decisions. . . .

Dr. Yoshihiko Fujikawa, a resident of Terminal Island, described the scene prior to evacuation:

'It was during these 48 hours that I witnessed unscrupulous vultures in the form of human beings taking advantage of bewildered housewives. . . . These were offered pittances for practically new furniture and appliances: refrigerators, radio consoles, etc., as well as cars, and many were falling prey to these people.'

The day after evacuation, Terminal Island was littered with abandoned household goods and equipment."

anti-Oriental movements on the West Coast, and the pressures, rumors, and fears that had led to the evacuation."[49]

CIVILIAN EXCLUSION ORDERS

While the WRA made its preparations, the army began posting the first instructions regarding evacuation. Beginning on March 24, 1942, and continuing through June, Civilian Exclusion Orders were stuck in shop windows and on telephone poles, informing all persons of Japanese American ancestry that they should be ready to move by a certain date, usually within a week. One observer remarked,

> As we went down California Street (in San Francisco) on the cable car . . . we saw soldiers nailing the evacuation orders onto telegraph poles at each street corner . . . the word "Japanese" (was) written large so that it was visible from across the street. I couldn't help thinking of Munich [Germany] in 1936 when the posters appeared overnight on the walls of buildings along the street, proclaiming various restrictions for Jews.[50]

Japanese were also directed to report to a civil control station (usually a public building in their community) where they were registered and given an identification number. They were known by that number throughout their internment. One woman later wrote, "Henry went to the control station to register the family. He came home with twenty tags, all numbered 10710, tags to be attached to each

piece of baggage, and one to hang from our coat lapels. From then on, we were known as family #10710."[51]

At registration centers, families were also told what they could bring to camp. Provisions were to include nothing but bedding, toilet articles, extra clothes, tableware, and a few personal effects. No one was told where they were going or how long they would be gone, so it was difficult to know how much to pack or what kinds of clothes would be needed.

"TAKE IT OR LEAVE IT"

After registration, families had dozens of decisions to make in a short period of

Seattle police post Civilian Exclusion Orders on city light poles in June 1942.

time. Homes, businesses, vehicles, pets, and household goods had to be sold, stored, or given away. Evacuees were assured by the government that no one would have to sacrifice any valuable personal property, and federal reserve banks in San Francisco, Los Angeles, Seattle, and Portland were made custodians for automobiles, furniture, and the like. The Farm Security Administration was in charge of care for evacuees' farm property and equipment during their absence.

Most evacuees did not take advantage of government programs, however. Worried about the need for money, most were inclined to sell everything as quickly as they could for whatever they could get. This created a buyer's market, and unscrupulous dealers often preyed on those who were desperate. One evacuee stated, "People who were like vultures swooped down on us, going through our belongings offering us a fraction of their value. When we complained to them of the low price they would respond by saying, 'you can't take it with you so take it or leave it.'"[52]

Many property owners leased their land; others sold it outright. Those who were raising crops usually had to leave them in the fields for others to harvest. One man wrote, "In northern California they let the Japanese put in all their crops. Then about three days before harvest, when the Japanese had put in all the work and money, they discovered a 'military necessity' and evacuated them. Others got the benefit of their investment and efforts."[53]

Not every Caucasian was ready to take advantage of the evacuees' predicament,

however. Friends and neighbors willingly agreed to oversee land and/or store personal possessions while families were gone. One evacuee wrote, "I gave my pictures to the camera club friends, the piano I put into the church parlor, the washing machine and dishes went into the basement of one friend, the books into the basement of another friend. Here and there our boxes were scattered all over the town."[54]

TIME TO GO

Evacuation Day, called E-Day by many, was a time of great stress for most families. Told to report to control centers, they conscientiously gathered ahead of time with their suitcases, boxes, and bags. Everyone was nervous and uncertain about what to expect. Volunteers from neighborhood churches tried to ease the strain by helping with children, by handing out coffee and doughnuts, and by driving the sick and aged so they would not have to make an arduous bus or train ride to an assembly center.

Evacuees appreciated such kindness, but the confusion, anxiety, and sadness made it a horrible day for most. Nearly everyone tried to hide their unhappiness behind a joke or a polite smile. Onlookers such as one volunteer from Seattle were impressed with their dignity and patience. He wrote,

This afternoon the first trainload of Japanese . . . left for Pinedale, California. I was down to see them off, and my heart split wider than it has for

Each member of the Mochida family of Hayward, California, wear their identification tags as they wait for the bus to evacuate them to an assembly center.

any of the others at the time of departure. No Pullmans [railroad sleeping cars] this time. . . . Just old ratty coaches for a 2 day, 2 night trip to California. . . . The Japanese were their cheerful selves: stoicism is a wonderful thing for circumstances like these.[55]

Not everyone was long-suffering or cooperative. At least one man went into hiding and was not found for three weeks. Californian Fred Korematsu, who later challenged the constitutionality of evacuation and internment in court,

avoided the process for a time by posing as a Spanish Hawaiian. At least two people committed suicide rather than endure the shame. One of these was World War I–veteran Hideo Murata, an Issei who had been given an honorary citizenship award for his contributions during that earlier conflict. When Murata learned that the evacuation orders were not "a mistake, or perhaps just a practical joke,"[56] he got a room in a local hotel, went inside, and took his life. He was later found with his certificate of honorary citizenship clutched in his hand.

ASSEMBLY CENTERS

After evacuees were processed, the mood of the day became even grimmer. Everyone was loaded aboard buses and trains under the watchful eye of armed military guards. Windows were often covered with paper to prevent anyone from seeing the countryside through which they passed, a circumstance that reinforced the feeling that they were prisoners. One evacuee remembered, "We got on, and as

UNDER ORDERS

It was common for a wide range of visitors to gather on weekends to see friends at assembly centers such as Camp Harmony in Puyallup, Washington. Although the atmosphere was usually relaxed, author Anne Reeploeg Fisher got a hint of what internees went through as they coped with repressive and unpredictable rules and regulations. Her account is given in Exile of a Race.

"As the chill spring of 1942 turned into summer, more and more visitors began coming to Camp Harmony. Every Sunday afternoon we found clusters of people alongside the fence—mainly Caucasians on the outside and their friends on the inside. Tension had eased and the guards relaxed their suspicious vigilance. . . .

As we sat beside the fence we saw all types of visitors: A Negro in chauffer's (sic) uniform who drove down in his employer's expensive car; a Filipino who had taken over the farm of his employer, coming down to make a report; high school and university students bringing packages down to their classmates. There was a skid road character with unkempt appearance and a devil-may-care glint in his eye. Out from the mess hall bounced a plump Japanese wearing the white cap and coat of a cook. They shook hands and whispered together, then when the guard turned his back, the unkempt one quickly slipped the cook a flask of whiskey. The cook hid it under his coat and then they turned and winked at us and laughed like a couple of kids who had put something over on the teacher. . . .

When we arrived the following Sunday the regulations had been changed and the friendly guards were all gone. . . . We were required to fill out forms giving our names and addresses, the names of persons we wished to see and why we wished to see them. There were long lines of puzzled visitors and to questions the only answer was 'new orders.'"

we traveled, I noticed that wherever we hit a town, the MPs [military police] would tell us to pull the shades down and we'd be curious, because we didn't know where we were going."[57]

About eighteen thousand evacuees went directly to the Manzanar relocation center in southern California and the Poston relocation center in Arizona since both facilities were virtually completed. (Manzanar was both an assembly and a relocation center.) The rest went to fifteen temporary assembly centers that were set up in Washington, Oregon, and California. The centers were operative only about seven months—until relocation camps were built and residents were transferred to permanent quarters—and the average stay for an evacuee was about one hundred days.

Assembly centers were not the worst that evacuees had feared when they left their homes. Neither were they comfortable or homelike, however. They were usually set up at fairgrounds, racetracks, or other public sites that were equipped with water, electricity, and bathroom facilities and could hold large numbers of people. High barbed-wire fences were erected around the perimeter to guarantee that no one could get in or out. One historian writes, "What struck most of the internees was the sudden horror of the watchtowers, the soldiers with bared bayonets, the searchlights at night ceaselessly playing over the grounds."[58]

New arrivals discovered that living conditions were primitive at best. Grandstands, display halls, and livestock stables were converted into tiny one-room apartments, which had to hold an entire family. The only furnishings were cots and a kerosene or wood stove. During bad weather, buildings were drafty and cold.

The owner of this grocery in Oakland put up "I AM AN AMERICAN" the day after Pearl Harbor. With the exclusion order he had to leave, and sold his business for much less than it was worth.

Anxious Japanese American citizens forced out of their homes in Los Angeles wait to board a train bound for the relocation center at Manzanar.

On sunny days, temperatures climbed and the smell of animals was overpowering. One evacuee described conditions in the "dormitory"—a room under the grandstand of one fairground where single men were housed. "There are about 500 men in there and when they all take their shoes off, the odor that greets you is terrific. What a stench!"[59]

In Camp Harmony, an assembly center at the fairgrounds in Puyallup, Washington, some residents were housed in squatty, windowless shacks (constructed in parking lots) that resembled rabbit hutches or chicken coops. "They sure go in for poultry in a big way here,"[60] one evacuee commented as the bus turned into the center grounds. Inside, ceilings were low and light came from a single bulb hanging from the ceiling. None of the rooms had heat, and water was available from bathrooms and laundry rooms some distance away. One evacuee joked,

"There is running water in every apartment, that is, you do the running . . . and hope that the water is still hot by the time you reach your . . . apartment."[61]

THE INSULT OF INCARCERATION

Evacuees were reminded that they were prisoners in dozens of ways. Upon entering the centers, belongings were inspected and men were "frisked." Camp searches occurred any time of the day or night and suspicious articles that ranged from baseball bats to books of Japanese poetry were confiscated. Curfews kept everyone in their barracks at night; even bathroom visits after 9:00 P.M. were forbidden. Rules were strict and arbitrary. Some camps allowed women to keep knitting needles, but others did not. In at least one case when internees complained that they were not receiving packages that

Living conditions at the assembly centers were primitive, stark, and restrictive.

had been sent to them from friends outside, administrators threatened to stop deliveries entirely.

Army soldiers, who acted as guards and sentries, were a constant presence. Although guards were ostensibly there to protect the Japanese from hostile persons on the outside, their actions proved otherwise. For instance, when a soldier saw a shadowy shape moving outside a fence one night, he commanded it to halt, then shot it. The offender turned out to be a cow. As one evacuee observed, "It could have been a child . . . a twelve-year-old out on a spree."[62]

SERIOUS SHORTCOMINGS

Sanitary conditions were poor in the centers, despite the fact that the army claimed the opposite. Flies were everywhere. Mud was a serious problem when it rained. Plumbing in bathrooms and laundries backed up from overuse. Improperly prepared food caused food poisoning. One report turned in by the army's quartermaster corps officer stated, "The kitchens are not up to Army standards of cleanliness. . . . The dishes looked bad . . . gray and cracked. . . . Dishwashing not very satisfactory due to an insufficiency of hot water. . . . Soup plates being used instead of plates, which means that the food all runs together and looks untidy and unappetizing."[63] The fact that food was often served out of (clean) garbage cans and dishpans added to evacuees' disgust since they, by tradition, served beautifully arranged food, usually on individual plates.

Those who became sick or were injured in accidents realized that serious shortcomings existed when it came to medical care as well. Even with the help of Japanese health-care workers who offered their services, often only three or four doctors and a handful of nurses cared for thousands of people. Shortages of equipment and medicine made treatment difficult, although everyone did the best he or she could under the circumstances. Those patients who were known to be severely ill were usually transferred to nearby community hospitals, but internee doctors treated injuries, delivered babies, and coped with mini-epidemics of viruses and childhood illnesses during their time in the centers.

COMMUNAL LIFE

Throughout internment, people were housed side by side with no regard for background or social status. Old and

---

GOOD MEN

Although the War Relocation Authority (WRA) played a role in holding internees captive, it also had as two of its goals their humane treatment and their rapid resettlement out of the camps. It did reasonably well in both regards due to the efforts of its two national directors, Milton Eisenhower and Dillon Myer. Author Page Smith describes them in Democracy on Trial.

"[The first WRA director was] the humane and intelligent Milton Eisenhower, who did his best to avoid setting up the centers at all, and, once the necessity of doing so was inescapable (in the sense that evacuation had been ordered and places had to be found for people to go), made it the goal of the War Relocation Authority to get out of business as soon as possible by resettling, or 'relocating,' evacuees out of the centers.

Dillon Myer carried on in the same spirit. . . . He was the most vocal and eloquent defender of the evacuees. He expended himself without stint to testify before hostile Senate and House subcommittees. He visited the centers repeatedly to explain and defend his policies . . . not to mention speaking before innumerable Chambers of Commerce, gatherings of World War I veterans, skeptical service club gatherings, and, indeed, to anyone who cared to listen. . . . The best testimony to his accomplishments was the esteem in which most of the evacuees subsequently held the man who had presided over their destiny for some three and a half years. . . . Even the bitterest critics of the evacuation acknowledged that he was a 'good man.'"

young, professional and laborer, Christian and Buddhist, liberal and conservative—all tolerated the same sleeping accommodations, ate the same food, and coped with the same lack of privacy. Every moment of the day and night was shared. Arguments, babies crying, people snoring—all rang in the ears of everyone crammed together in the make-do living quarters.

Meals were eaten in communal halls that were noisy and crowded. Showers were communal as well, and older Issei who were used to the luxury of a hot bath at the end of the day now had to stand shoulder to shoulder with strangers in an open room if they wanted to wash. Communal toilets were more traumatic than

the showers. Arranged in long rows, back to back, toilets were set up in the middle of the room with no partitions between. A woman in a Merced, California, center wrote, "The toilets are one big row of seats, that is, one straight board with holes out about a foot apart with no partitions at all and all the toilets flush together . . . about every five minutes. The younger girls couldn't go to them at first until they couldn't stand it any longer, which is really bad for them."[64]

Evacuees tried to solve their privacy problems by holding up newspapers that they pretended to read. Eventually, many used portable curtains or cardboard partitions that offered a small amount of privacy.

Armed guards and sentries, poor sanitary conditions, inadequate medical care, and barbed, wire fences were the shocking reality of the assembly centers.

THE STRAIN OF UNCERTAINTY

It was difficult for most evacuees to adjust to life in the assembly centers, particularly because they did not know what the future would bring. Historian Anne Reeploeg Fisher writes, "Buffeted and insulted, hurt and despairing, many evacuees' faith in America was fading. Many saw no hope for a decent future in the United States where fair play seemed to be reserved for white citizens."[65]

The government did not seem to care about how the evacuees were feeling. Official announcements were rare, so rumors ran rampant: everyone was going to be released, everyone was going to be sent to Japan, everyone was going to be sent into some remote wilderness and forgotten. False stories of rapes and shootings in the centers caused many Japanese

Residents of Camp Harmony Assembly Center in Puyallup, Washington, had to line up outside in the weather three times a day for meals.

to live in terror. News accounts of anti-Japanese hostility on the outside left many thinking that they had no good options in or out of the centers.

A few outsiders understood the strain of living in such a state of uncertainty, but their efforts to help were necessarily limited. For instance, a group of Quakers who had visited the Minidoka relocation center in Idaho made a point of reporting back to residents of Camp Harmony Assembly Center in Puyallup. Their description of barracks set among sagebrush and lava rock was daunting, but to residents it was better than total ignorance. "If you could have seen their faces beam to have some real first-hand news from the outside world of what is happening beyond the barbed wire,"[66] one Quaker stated.

Despite hardships and humiliation, evacuees tried to make the best of their new lives. They made new friends, settled into their tiny apartments, and established new routines. Just as they did, however, another disturbing announcement was made. Relocation centers had been completed. The process of moving would begin again.

Once again, rumors were rampant and fears multiplied. Families worried that they might be separated. No one knew whether to pack or wait until they received instructions. Messages from those who went first and reported back sometimes made matters worse. For instance, a letter from Arizona that circulated through one assembly center stated, "This HELL on earth is absolutely not a fit place for human beings. . . . I urgently advise you to ask to be sent to Tule Lake [California] or some other area of temperate climate."[67]

There seemed to be no end to the trauma, and nothing ahead but a frightening future.

4 Behind Barbed Wire

By June 1942 residents were being transferred into permanent WRA relocation centers throughout the West. Everyone was relieved to find that these camps were not brutal concentration camps like those established by the Nazis in Europe, but they were prisons nevertheless, stark, restrictive, and uncomfortable.

Ironically, romanticized stories of the camps flourished on the outside. Press coverage of First Lady Eleanor Roosevelt's visit to the Gila River center—a showplace camp—emphasized its gardens (maintained by camp residents), picturesque streets, and vine-covered porches that some internees built outside their barrack-homes. Manzanar, in southern California, was set against the backdrop of the Sierra Nevada mountains, and photographs captured the romance of the locale while ignoring the physical hardships, mental cruelties, and the lack of freedom that internees experienced.

First Lady Eleanor Roosevelt's visit to the Gila River relocation center was designed to show the public the beauty of the location and the happy life of the internees.

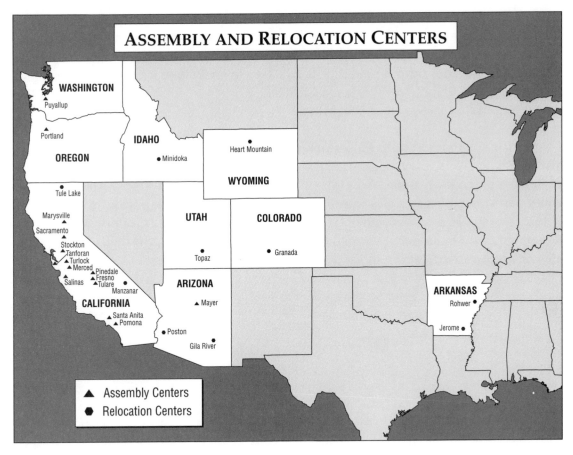

ASSEMBLY AND RELOCATION CENTERS

WASHINGTON
▲ Puyallup

▲ Portland

IDAHO
● Minidoka

OREGON

WYOMING
● Heart Mountain

▲ Tule Lake

UTAH
● Topaz

COLORADO
● Granada

▲ Marysville
▲ Sacramento
▲ Stockton
▲ Tanforan
▲ Turlock
▲ Merced
▲ Pinedale
▲ Fresno
▲ Salinas ▲ Tulare
● Manzanar

ARIZONA
▲ Mayer

CALIFORNIA
▲ Santa Anita
▲ Pomona
● Poston
Gila River

ARKANSAS
Rohwer ●

Jerome ●

▲ Assembly Centers
● Relocation Centers

REMOTE AND TERRIBLE

In selecting sites for the centers, the WRA had followed four guidelines. Construction needed to be on federal land. Each center had to be large enough to hold at least five thousand people. All sites had to be safely distant from strategic points such as military bases and cities with industry. All had to be close enough to civilization so they could be supplied by utilities such as power and water. By the second week of June, sites for ten centers had been chosen—two each in California, Arizona, and Arkansas, and one each in Idaho, Wyoming, Utah, and Colorado.

Not only were the settings remote, but the climate of the camps was often harsh. Jerome and Rohwer centers in Arkansas were built on swampland infested with malarial mosquitoes. Tule Lake, California; Minidoka, Idaho; and Heart Mountain, Wyoming, experienced severe winters. Temperatures at Topaz in Utah and Poston in Arizona rose well above one hundred degrees in the summer. Since the army had bulldozed away all vegetation in preparation for construction, residents at many of the camps endured terrible dust storms when the wind blew. One resident at Manzanar in southern California wrote, "It was . . .

when our eyes became bloodshot with the fine dust, our throats parched, and I suppose our reason a little obtuse [dull], that we fell into the common practice of trying to figure out just how in the world we would find our way out of this man-made hell."[68]

On each site, barbed-wire fences and guard towers were erected around the perimeter. Barracks, fire stations, storage warehouses, and other facilities were built within. Most buildings consisted of tar paper and uncured boards that warped and shrank as they dried, letting in sand and dirt. Barracks were arranged with military precision into blocks of twenty-four each. Four blocks formed a ward, and there were usually nine wards per center.

RISING TO THE CHALLENGE

Living conditions were generally better in the camps than in the assembly centers. Buildings were new, and there was more space on the grounds so residents could get away from their ever-present neighbors. Nevertheless, conditions

---

MONOTONOUS AND BORING

Life in most relocation camps was purposeless and frustrating for many, and it led to unhappiness and wrangling among residents. One Nisei, a resident of the Gila River center in Arizona, describes the situation in Dorothy Swaine Thomas's The Salvage.

"The Gila life was pretty monotonous and boring at times and it didn't seem to lead anywhere. I had to think of a future beyond that because I had a baby and a wife for which I was responsible. I knew that I could not provide any sort of a future for them in camp. I felt I was just wasting my time there if I stayed too long. It seemed that the war was going to last for quite a while and I didn't want to stay in camp for three or four years. I had nothing against the WRA. They did as well as they could considering all the problems that they had. Naturally the Japanese people in camp were resentful about a lot of things and many of them were looking around for gripes. They just didn't care for the *hakujins* [Caucasians] and they wanted to blame them for everything. There were all sorts of gripes about the food, barracks, dust, linoleum, clothing, and everything else. I don't know what all of the bickering was about because I wasn't in contact with any of it. I know they used to have a lot of block meetings to talk over these gripes but I never attended."

---

were still difficult and frustrating. Bathrooms, laundries, and dining halls were communal. Barracks were hot in summer and cold in winter. Space was at a premium; most apartments were about twenty feet by twenty feet square. Each was heated by a small oil-burning stove, and none had running water. The only furniture provided was a bed and two blankets per person. Residents were shown a pile of straw and had to stuff their own mattress ticking before they could sleep.

Residents were used to such challenges by now, however. As one WRA report stated, "The great majority of center residents were a psychologically bruised, badly puzzled and frequently apathetic group of people. But during their stay at the centers they . . . tried to achieve some semblance of order and dignity in their broken lives."[69]

Beginning with the basics, they swept the sand out of apartments and nailed tin-can lids over knotholes that let in drafts. Many made furniture out of scrap lumber. Most sewed curtains for privacy and to make rooms more homelike. In time, the WRA provided Drywall and linoleum to make rooms weatherproof and easier to keep clean.

Former farmers and gardeners began landscaping the barren ground around the barracks in an effort to soften the ugliness of the terrain. Internees planted flowers and greenery in front of their apartments. Some created landscaped parks complete with trees, lawns, and ponds where families could picnic and children could play.

DO-IT-YOURSELF

Although it was the responsibility of the WRA to provide essentials in the camps, its efforts often fell short of residents' standards. Institutional meals supplied by the army quartermaster corps provoked widespread complaints. Many of the residents were used to eating a traditional Japanese diet and objected to the "American" menu. Other residents hated the fact that food was unimaginative and unappetizing. One internee remembered her first dinner. "They issued us army mess kits, the round metal kind that fold over, and plopped in scoops of canned Vienna sausage, canned string beans, [and] steamed rice that had been cooked too long."[70] When internees dumped inedible food in the trash, authorities assumed portions were too large and cut back, creating further misery.

Residents quickly assumed much of the responsibility for meal preparation and food production. Farmers and laborers went to work plowing, planting, and producing crops such as cabbage, squash, tomatoes, and soybeans, which made up a large part of the Japanese diet. Some internees worked at raising poultry, hogs, and dairy cattle. Japanese cooks helped staff the kitchens and plan menus, and soon residents reported that meals were more tolerable with a variety of choices being offered.

Along with food production, some centers became involved in food processing. Manzanar made all of its own soy sauce, and tofu-making plants were a part of each camp. Also at Manzanar, guayule—a Southwestern shrub—was grown to help

Food was prepared and served in noisy, crowded mess halls.

combat a national rubber shortage caused by the war. Evacuee chemists worked on rubber extraction and production in makeshift laboratories. "For glassware we have accumulated some jam jars and we are eating peanut butter like mad so that we can use the jars that come with it,"[71] wrote one chemist. Experimenters were successful at producing a useable product at very low cost.

With a great deal of effort, internees soon created communities that resembled the outside world. Sympathetic friends on the outside helped supply en-

ergetic businessmen and women with goods they needed to establish small repair shops, beauty parlors, and dry-goods stores. Journalists started newspapers and newsletters. Boy and Girl Scout leaders continued troop activities. Teens scheduled dances and holiday celebrations. All who worked were paid wages by the WRA, although those wages were very low—about twelve to sixteen dollars per month for a forty-eight-hour workweek. In contrast, the average American soldier was paid between twenty and fifty dollars a month.

SELF-GOVERNMENT

Most internees were willing to cooperate and make camp life as tolerable as possible, but, as in all communities, some leadership was necessary. Each camp had its own Caucasian administrator and staff, who were, for the most part, businesslike individuals who tried to govern fairly and give residents as much freedom as possible. For instance, director Harry Stafford allowed the Minidoka, Idaho, Nisei baseball team to travel to Idaho Falls to play in the state championship at the end of one season. Guy Robertson, director at Heart Mountain, Wyoming, allowed internees to take sightseeing bus trips to Yellowstone Park. At Manzanar, a camp official noted, "The back gate of the camp was often open; the farm hands went freely in and out and [director Ralph] Merritt . . . looked with leniency upon recreational sorties [outings], since they were no danger to military security."[72]

Because of the number of people in the camps, however, spokespersons were needed to act as links between internees and staff. Many camps elected or appointed block managers—usually respected Issei—who supervised grounds maintenance, ensured that everyone had necessary provisions, and passed on official WRA announcements. Most camps also had community councils made up of young adult Nisei who spoke English well and were familiar with American

A young Los Angeles attorney and his family sit in their tiny living area at Manzanar.

ways. Their roles ranged from policy making to dealing with mild infractions of the law such as juvenile delinquency and petty theft. The WRA could veto any council decisions, however. This led many internees to feel that the system was only a maneuver to lull them into thinking they had some power.

HEALTH CARE

The inadequate health care that internees had experienced in assembly centers continued into camp life. Once again, Japanese American doctors, dentists, and nurses stepped forward to aid internees who needed treatment. Most of these professionals were overworked and underpaid. At Jerome, Arkansas, in late 1942,

for instance, seven doctors earning only sixteen dollars a month were on call to serve ten thousand residents. (The pay for professionals was later raised to nineteen dollars a month.)

In many cases medical personnel worked under conditions that would have alarmed health-care professionals on the outside. Camp hospitals were not completed until months after internees arrived, so everyone coped in makeshift clinics. Even when hospitals were finished, they lacked the necessities. One nurse at Tule Lake Relocation Center recalled, "I remember a pregnant woman came in with just terrible pain, . . . [and it was] absolutely necessary to operate right away. . . . But there was no doctor to do the surgery. The woman died of a hemorrhage without delivering her baby."[73]

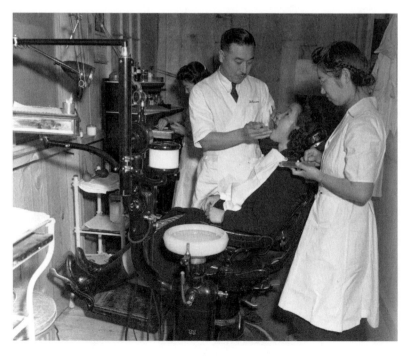

Japanese American dentists offered their services to fellow internees at Puyallup center.

Typhoid, tuberculosis, and dysentery were common at many camps. So were respiratory-tract infections and epidemics of childhood illnesses such as measles and chicken pox. Polio was a problem in the Granada (Colorado) camp; malaria sickened many residents in the Arkansas centers before a mosquito-eradication program was introduced.

"RISE HIGHER"

While resident health-care workers struggled to keep camp residents healthy, others worked to boost internees' mental and emotional well-being. Christian and Buddhist churches were a significant part of the camps from the start. Outreach groups from Catholic, Episcopalian, and Unitarian churches also offered support, and well-known religious leaders traveled from camp to camp, encouraging and counseling patience. One Nisei recalled the inspirational words of E. Stanley Jones, head of the Federal Council of Churches. "He talked about the eagle in Isaiah 40:31 and our experience. He said, 'Don't let this experience destroy you. Use it like an eagle to lift yourself up. The eagle doesn't go against the storm clouds, it uses them to rise higher, giving it strength and this is what you people will have to do so you won't be destroyed.'"[74]

Some of the most dedicated humanitarians were the Quakers, who not only led worship services but also provided necessities such as warm clothes, household supplies, and small luxuries. One Quaker missionary remembers, "It was on our first trip to Manzanar that I was asked to get the Yamamoto Dodge truck, and from that time I usually went up in that with loads of furniture, books, trunks, etc., for the internees. . . . The WRA would get these things, but it took weeks for each request to be carried through."[75]

The Quakers were quick to notice conditions that needed to be corrected or improved in the camps, and they pestered authorities until the problems were fixed. They also continually reminded authorities that internment was an unjust state of affairs. One historian comments, "Though a soft-spoken and gentle-mannered lot, the splendid Quakers did not mince words in their open criticism of the Army's raw abuse of power, a candor little appreciated by the military."[76]

STRUCTURE AND SCHOLARSHIP

Early in internment, education-minded internees organized schools to provide instruction and give structure to young people's lives. Shortly thereafter, the WRA hired Caucasian teachers to live in the camps and oversee educational efforts. Many of these outsiders were retired missionaries or conscientious objectors. Usually they worked side by side with volunteers and learned to appreciate their dedication and creativity.

Despite many good intentions, all camp schools suffered from serious shortcomings. Space was at a premium, so classes were overcrowded. Storms often forced teachers to send students home. Even on the best of days, a shortage of

BASEBALL AND MAH JONGG

With plenty of time on their hands, the most energetic center residents filled their days with work, family responsibilities, and recreation encouraged by the WRA. In Personal Justice Denied, *the report of the Commission on the Wartime Relocation and Internment of Civilians, some of the most popular pastimes are described.*

"Athletics were a major recreation. While the preferences of Issei and Nisei differed in most cases, baseball was a common denominator. At some centers, there were as many as 100 teams active at one time, ranging from children to Issei in their sixties. Basketball and touch football were popular as well. Indoor sports were limited to those that took little space—primarily ping-pong, judo, boxing and badminton. *Sumo* wrestling bouts were given for those interested in the traditional sports of Japan. By the end of 1943, evacuees were sometimes allowed to leave the grounds, so that hiking and swimming became popular pastimes.

The evacuees also diverted themselves with dancing, plays, concerts, and games—cards, chess, checkers, *Goh, Shogi* and *Mah jongg* [traditional Asian games]. Some activities were underwritten by outside groups—an art competition in 1943, for example, was sponsored by Massachusetts Quakers. There were numerous art or craft exhibitions and films that came to each mess hall. At Manzanar, an outdoor walk-in theatre was eventually built, where evacuees could see most current films."

Softball teams were very popular at Manzanar.

supplies—books, chairs, tables, black-boards, pencils, and paper—made teaching almost impossible. Dillon Myer recalled,

> All centers had some common problems such as teacher recruitment, training, and supervision, as well as the need to utilize temporary and inadequate quarters and equipment during the early months. In spite of all of these frustrations, however, the schools did an amazingly good job under very difficult conditions—thanks to the interest generally shown among the students and their parents, and the dedication of the teachers, including evacuees who served full time as assistant teachers.[77]

The obstacles were great, but thousands of Japanese American students attended camp schools, and many graduated during internment. The most motivated then went on to college under the WRA's student relocation plan. Unfortunately, the stress of internment proved so unsettling for some children that they lost their enthusiasm for learning. Problems that had seldom cropped up in the Japanese American community before—cheating, bullying, vandalism, and disrespectful attitudes—became more common. The San Francisco *Chronicle* reported in May 1943, "Two-thirds—the younger, American-born and American-citizen Nisei—are becoming increasingly bitter, resentful and even sullen."[78] Dissatisfaction among residents increased when it became known that the WRA was improving staff living quarters rather than purchasing equipment it had promised the schools.

Crowded classroom such as this one at the Minidoka relocation center were often run by Caucasian volunteers. The schoolroom furniture was built by the parents in camp shops.

TROUBLE IN THE CENTERS

Discontent and disagreements were inevitable in the camps because of the variety of people who were interned and the grim conditions under which they had to live.

Anyone who worked with the administration came under criticism since they were seen as collaborating with the WRA. In some cases, residents did inform on each other and thus justified suspicions. As one official stated, "The administration were *inu* [dogs] . . . and the evacuees who cooperated were called worse."[79]

Another source of discontent was the difference in privileges that different groups enjoyed. For instance, the Nisei, being citizens, were often given more responsibility and freedom than the Issei and the Kibei, with resulting resentment and division. Generational disputes also arose as Nisei sons assumed leadership and Issei fathers lost authority they had once taken for granted.

Sometimes differences arose simply because of regional differences in background. One historian writes, "At Manzanar, Terminal Islanders, a vociferous, tight-knit group, clashed with people from West Los Angeles and Bainbridge Island [Washington]. The Northwesterners at Manzanar found the Californians 'very Oriental.'"[80]

Poor living conditions and unfair treatment usually stirred up the most serious trouble. Such was the case at Poston in November 1942 when, according to one historian, "heat, dust, primitive facilities, broken promises and factional [group] conflict"[81] led to a strike of all workers in camp. The strike concluded when administration and residents reached a compromise and residents were promised greater involvement in future camp decision making.

Manzanar was the site of one of the worst revolts in late 1942. Tensions were high as a result of food shortages, rumored to be caused by dishonest Caucasian cooks. The activities of informers added to the problem. On December 5 a group of men led by Joe Kurihara attacked one of these informers, a Japanese American Citizens League leader. When some of the assailants were taken into custody, Kurihara urged a takeover of the camp, and director Ralph Merritt was forced to declare martial law. Military police were called in, shots were fired, and two people were killed. Tension eased only after ringleaders were removed to a Justice Department camp in Leupp, Arizona.

Other flare-ups occurred in the Topaz camp in March 1943 and in the Tule Lake camp in October that same year. During the latter incident, some of the Caucasian staff feared for their safety. When the episode was over, a few gave eyewitness accounts to West Coast newspapers. Sensational accounts of riots and hostage-taking followed, leading the outside world to believe that the camps were chaotic places, that the WRA had lost control, and that the Army needed to "crack down" on Japanese Americans. "We felt that under the Army we had a better chance . . . of getting proper discipline and a proper segregation than we have under the existing set up,"[82] explained Senator Mon C. Wallgren of Washington.

GREATER ISOLATION

Contrary to outside opinion, residents who stirred up trouble in the camps were usually not tolerated for long. Most were arrested by military police and, if they were citizens, were transported to WRA isolation camps located in Moab, Utah, or Leupp, Arizona. Disruptive aliens were taken to Justice Department internment camps located in Santa Fe, New Mexico; Bismarck, North Dakota; Missoula, Montana; or Crystal City, Texas. There, they joined suspect German and Italian Americans, those Japanese who had been arrested by the FBI shortly after Pearl Harbor, and Japanese deportees from Central and South America. (The United States accepted the latter, then exchanged them with Japan for Americans trapped in Japanese-controlled territory.)

Conditions in isolation and Justice Department camps were much the same as in mainstream WRA relocation camps. All internees were housed in barracks, fed an adequate diet, and allowed to participate in work programs, recreation, education, and the like. At Center City, some women and children even joined husbands and fathers, although most men did not experience this luxury.

Moab camp, established by Raymond Best, a U.S. Marine Corps veteran who would later head up Tule Lake Segregation Center, was an exception to the others. At Moab, rules were rigid and dehumanizing, mail was censored, men were under constant supervision, and guards were under orders to shoot to kill. Fortunately, Moab was closed in early 1943, and inmates were moved to Leupp. There, under the humane direction of Paul Robertson, conditions mirrored other camps and prisoners had greater freedom. Leupp itself closed in December 1943, when Tule Lake Segregation Center was established.

CANADA, ALASKA, AND HAWAII

The United States was not the only country to believe that the segregation and control of Japanese Americans was vital to national security. In Canada and the Alaska Territory, all Japanese were interned in camps much like those that were set up in the United States.

Ironically, Japanese Americans in the U.S. territory of Hawaii were not imprisoned, despite the fact that Hawaii was deep in the war zone. There were several reasons for this: Hawaiians were more racially tolerant, there was no evidence that Japanese Americans had been in any way responsible for the bombing of Pearl Harbor, and the Japanese made up a large proportion of the workforce. Incarcerating them would have had a disastrous effect on the local economy. Thus, they were allowed to remain in their homes and work throughout the course of the war.

A WAY OUT

Life in the camps was difficult, and the Japanese longed for the day internment would end. Fortunately for them, Dillon Myer also believed that their stay should be as short as possible. He supported a re-settlement process that began even before some of the camps opened. A prerequisite to leaving, however, was that all internees had to show that they would not be a danger to society and that they had a specific place to go. Myer explained, "The WRA leave policy, which provided . . . that evacuees must have clearance to leave the centers was decided for two reasons—first, to assure the American public that relocatees were not dangerous—and, secondly, for the protection of the evacuees themselves in view of the stigma caused by the mass evacuation."[83]

Whether the WRA cared for their welfare or not, the leave programs offered a way out. That was all that many Japanese Americans cared about. The outside world was too full of possibilities for them to linger behind barbed wire any longer than necessary.

5 A Question of Loyalty

Getting out of the camps came down to a question of loyalty, a quality that people like General John DeWitt felt was impossible to determine in Japanese Americans. WRA director Dillon Myer disagreed with DeWitt. In his view, the camps were "way-stations for persons willing to resettle in other parts of the United States,"[84] and he relied on references and the internees' personal histories in clearing the way for them to leave. Needless to say, those who wanted to get out were thoroughly scrutinized. One historian writes, "The evacuees may well have been the most investigated group of people in the history of the United States."[85]

SEASONAL LEAVE

Seasonal agricultural leave was one of the first and easiest ways to relocate out of a center. During 1942 a critical shortage of farmworkers developed in several western

Internees from the Granada relocation camp in Colorado worked to harvest the onion crop in 1942.

states because so many men had gone to fight in the war. Landowners were desperate for help in the fields. Thus, shortly after internment began state authorities who had pushed to get the Japanese into camps reluctantly reversed their position. They requested that some of the most able-bodied be recruited to do seasonal farm labor.

Internees were at first reluctant to volunteer for such a plan. They feared that they would be used as slave labor. Under terms of the program, however, their safety was guaranteed. Employers also had to pay reasonable wages and provide adequate housing.

After a small group of men went out on an exploratory visit in May 1942 and reported back that working and living conditions seemed acceptable, others agreed to take part. "It was an opportunity for the farmers and *hakujins* (white folk) out there because they were looking for cheap labor. . . . We saw it as an opportunity to get to go to the store and to buy stuff to bring back to the family,"[86] one said.

Despite guarantees, farmworkers often put up with poor living conditions for the weeks they spent out of camp. One reported, "Our living quarters was a shack without running water, heated by a coal stove, and we had to bathe in a ditch."[87] People in surrounding communities expressed serious concerns about having Japanese "running free" in their neighborhoods, and incidents of violence occurred. In one town, police officers beat an internee as he was returning to camp. In another area, local troublemakers harassed several teenage farmworkers by forcing them to crawl through a city park.

Internees who took advantage of the leave program were good workers and were willing to please, however, so hostility waned and demand grew. By mid-October 1942, ten thousand internees were taking advantage of seasonal leave, and the Nisei were credited with saving the sugar-beet crop in several western states that year.

STUDENT LEAVE

While some internees worked as farm laborers, others found a way out of the camps by pursuing their education. Almost twenty-five hundred young Nisei had been in colleges and universities when internment began, and educators such as Robert Gordon Sproul, president of the University of California, and Lee Paul Sieg, president of the University of Washington, expressed concern that internment might permanently damage their futures.

Through the efforts of these men and other private organizations, the National Japanese American Student Relocation Council was formed in early 1942. Steps were taken to find colleges and universities outside the evacuated area that would accept qualified internees. Almost 150 institutions, including Swarthmore College in Pennsylvania, the Universities of Nebraska and Texas, Radcliffe College in Massachusetts, and Oberlin Conservatory of Music in Ohio, agreed. Letters of references from teachers and professors on the West Coast usually guaranteed the students' good character, and the WRA granted about 250 educational leaves for

RESETTLEMENT

One of the primary goals of the WRA was out-of-center relocation—resettling internees in locales across the country where they could enjoy freedom and a normal way of life. In his book Uprooted Americans: The Japanese Americans and the War Relocation Authority, *WRA director Dillon S. Myer explains why he believed that rapid relocation was essential for both internees and the nation.*

"1. We recognized that loyalty could not flourish in an atmosphere of restriction and discriminatory segregation.

2. It was recognized that such a wide and enforced deviation from normal cultural and living patterns might very well have lasting and unfavorable effects upon individuals, particularly children and young people, who made up a large part of the population.

3. There was an obligation on the part of the War Relocation Authority both to the evacuees and to the people of the United States generally to restore all loyal citizens and law-abiding aliens to a normal useful American life with all possible speed.

4. Confinement in relocation centers fostered suspicion of evacuee loyalties and added to evacuee discouragements.

5. We did not want to be responsible for fostering a new set of reservations in the United States akin to Indian reservations."

the fall of 1942. Before the war ended, over 4,000 Nisei were in colleges and universities throughout the United States.

Most students had positive experiences on their new campuses, but some experienced obstacles. In an incident known as "the Battle of Parksville," the mayor and members of the American Legion in Parksville, Missouri, protested the admission of seven internee students set to start classes at nearby Parks College. The president of the college, backed by the student body, stood firm in his acceptance of the

newcomers, however, and the protests eventually ended.

The "Retreat from Moscow" was not a victory for internees. Upon their arrival at the University of Idaho in Moscow in the spring of 1942, eight students were informed that their admissions had been canceled, again because of local hostility. Intimidated by townspeople who threatened mob violence and even lynching, at least two female students took refuge in the local jail before returning to the camps.

Given a chance, students adjusted well to their new settings, performed well in school, and earned the friendship and respect of their professors and their peers. They also discovered that leaving the West Coast broadened their horizons and gave them the opportunity to interact with society as individuals rather than as members of a tight-knit racial group. "In this way I knew who I was . . . and how I fit into an American community and American history,"[88] one student stated.

Voluntary Enlistment

In one of the most commendable displays of loyalty shown during the war, thousands of young Nisei went straight from the camps to fight in Europe and the Pacific. Former senator S. I. Hayakawa says, "Since their words would not have been believed, especially in wartime, (they) communicated by action and behavior. 'We are good Americans,' they said. . . . 'We are useful and productive citizens. We love America and are willing to die for her.'"[89]

Many had assumed when the nation went to war in 1941 that they would be able to fight for their country. The government's rejection of them at that time was both disappointing and infuriating. Then, beginning in early 1943, Secretary of War Stimson was persuaded to reverse his policy and allowed Nisei to enlist. "It is the inherent right of every citizen, regardless of ancestry, to bear arms in the Nation's battle,"[90] he stated. An all-Nisei unit was created, and each qualified man who was judged a loyal citizen of the United States was allowed to serve.

The segregated makeup of the unit offended many Nisei, who saw it as another expression of discrimination. Some Nisei

The Yonemitsu family at Manzanar was proud of their son in the U.S. Army. About thirty-three thousand Japanese Americans served in the U.S. military during World War II.

were also offended because they had to complete a loyalty questionnaire before enlistment. Others decided they could not join because they would be separated from family members. They had become heads of the household in camp and worried about what would happen if they were not there to oversee things. At least a few men, such as a group at Heart Mountain in Wyoming, feared they were just being used. "The minds of us are still shrouded in doubt and confusion as to the true motives of our government when they invite our voluntary enlistment at the present time. It has not been explained why some American citizens, who patriotically volunteered, at the beginning of the war, were rejected by the Army."[91]

So strongly did some object that they refused to serve even when Stimson initiated a draft for Nisei in 1944. Refusal resulted in prosecution for some. At Heart Mountain, a total of eighty-five Nisei were tried and convicted of draft resistance and were sentenced to terms in federal penitentiaries. (Those who were convicted were granted a presidential pardon in 1947.) Ironically, their fellow Nisei were the harshest critics of their stand. "These men are fascists in my estimation and no good to any country," commented one Nisei veteran. "They have torn down (what) all the rest of us have tried to do."[92]

"YOU HAVE FOUGHT AND YOU HAVE WON"

Eventually a total of about thirty-three thousand Japanese Americans served in the U.S. military during World War II as medics, mechanics, language instructors, and in the Women's Army Corps (WACs). One Nisei became an air force gunner and flew bombing missions over Tokyo. A little-known group did intelligence work in the Pacific, serving as scouts, translators, and interpreters. Many of them had to attend language school before beginning their service since they were not fluent in Japanese, but they willingly learned the language to help ensure an Allied victory. Some of their achievements included providing a complete listing of the Japanese navy's ships, air squadrons, and bases. They also supplied the translation of Japan's entire battle plan for the defense of the Philippine Islands.

Those who served in the all-Nisei 442nd Regimental Combat Team took as their motto "Go for broke," and distinguished themselves by their courage and heroism. Their most celebrated accomplishment was saving the "Lost Battalion," a Texas unit in France that had been pinned down by the enemy for over a week. Eight hundred Nisei were killed or wounded in the battle; their casualties totaled more than the number of men they rescued. The 442nd eventually became one of the U.S. Army's most decorated units during World War II, earning over eighteen thousand individual decorations. WRA director Dillon Myer wrote, "The record of the segregated combat team stood out like a beacon on a dark night."[93]

The acts of Nisei servicemen and women were key to convincing America that Japanese Americans were sincere in their allegiance to the United States. Their heroic performance helped reverse public opinion and made relocation back into communities on the West Coast easier. On July 15, 1946, President Harry Truman honored the contributions of the 442nd at a White House ceremony and put their accomplishments into words: "You fought not only the enemy, but you fought prejudice and you have won."[94]

THE LOYALTY QUESTIONNAIRE

In mid-November 1942 the WRA reorganized so that it could more efficiently assist with out-of-center resettlement. It established a number of field offices in various large cities to help speed the process. It began promoting the idea of "indefinite leave" for internees who could find jobs in business and industry throughout the country and thus leave the camps permanently. According to Myer, "[WRA officers] met with employers individually and in groups, enlisted the aid of unions, and spoke to employees in plants where the employment of Japanese was contemplated."[95]

As a part of those efforts, the WRA proposed that all persons over the age of seventeen fill out a questionnaire entitled

The all-Nisei 442nd Regimental Combat Team was one of the army's most decorated units in World War II.

"Application for Leave Clearance." This was in essence the same loyalty form that was issued to potential military volunteers, but no one stopped to evaluate how internees of all ages and backgrounds would interpret the questions. No one thought to tell them the purpose of the program or how their responses would be used. As a result, instead of speeding up releases, the loyalty questionnaire became one of the most divisive, traumatic experiences of the internment period.

The four-page document asked about an internee's background—whether he or she was an American citizen, had ever been in Japan, had ever served in the Japanese military, had ever considered repatriating (moving) to Japan. Although most questions were straightforward, questions 27 and 28 produced much confusion and resentment. The former asked, "Are you willing to serve in the armed forces of the United States in combat duty?" (Women were asked if they would join the WACs or the Army Nurse Corps.) Question 28 asked, "Will you swear unqualified allegiance to the United States of America and forswear [give up] any form of allegiance or obedience to the Japanese emperor?"[96]

Internees were uncertain how to answer the questions for several reasons. First, they were being asked to swear loyalty and to serve in the military while they were being badly treated and denied their rights. Most felt that this was an unfair demand to make. Second, the Issei, who had not been allowed to become U.S. citizens, felt that if they renounced their Japanese citizenship they would become

people without a country. Finally, the Nisei objected to being asked to "give up" allegiance to Japan. They had always been loyal to the United States and thus had nothing to give up. They feared that question 28 was designed to trick them into appearing disloyal.

YES OR NO?

The way an internee answered questions 27 and 28 soon turned into an expression of his or her feelings about internment itself. Although most decided to trust the government and take the questions at face value, some marked "no" on their questionnaire in response to the aforementioned fears. Some answered "no" as a means of expressing their anger. Some followed the lead of other family members. In an ironic twist, some answered "no" in hopes of ensuring a more secure future. They feared that they would be forced out of the camps into the hostile world or made to go to war if they were cleared for leave.

For many, the decision was an agonizing one. Meetings were held with much discussion of the pros and cons. People took sides, and friends and family members who held differing views were divided. One internee reported, "The resulting infighting, beatings, and verbal abuses left families torn apart, parents against children, brothers against sisters. . . . So bitter was all this that even to this day, there are many amongst us who do not speak about that period."[97]

The questionnaire took on such importance that internees identified each other by the way they had answered. Those who had declared themselves willing to serve in the military and willing to renounce allegiance to Japan were termed "Yes-yeses." Those who refused were known as "No-noes."

SEGREGATION AT TULE LAKE

Internees' concerns were justified when the WRA labeled those who answered "no-no" as disloyal and began segregating them into another camp so they would not be a negative influence on loyal internees. Tule Lake in northern California was chosen as a segregation center since it had the largest proportion of disloyals when the questionnaires were tallied. In preparation for the camp's new status, a double fence was constructed around the entire area, the military guard was increased from two hundred to battalion strength (five hundred to twelve hundred men), and tanks were lined up in an impressive display of might.

CONTRIBUTIONS IN THE FIELDS

Doing seasonal agricultural work was much harder than remaining in a relocation center, but many internees preferred their freedom even at the price of backbreaking labor. As Roger Daniels points out in Concentration Camps, U.S.A.: Japanese Americans and World War II, *those internees were able to express their loyalty and willingness to contribute to the war effort through their hard work.*

"The contribution of the evacuees to the economy and the war effort was considerable. Leonard Arrington, the historian of the western beet sugar industry, has written of the experience of one large company with evacuee labor. Thanks largely to this labor the Utah-Idaho Sugar Company, one of the largest producers in the intermountain West, was able to increase its production from 72,000 acres in 1941 to 89,000 acres in 1942. Of the 10,000 Japanese workers on leave from Assembly Centers and Relocation Centers, the company was able to hire some 3,500, who, according to Arrington, 'were among the most industrious and intelligent workmen who ever labored in the region. One family of five, the Sakates of Delta, Utah, thinned 131 acres in the spring of 1942 and, in association with two other Nisei, topped, loaded and delivered 1,020 tons of beets during the period October 9 to November 10, 1942.' Altogether the evacuated people employed by this one company alone saved enough beets to make almost 100 million pounds of sugar, in itself a significant contribution to the war effort."

A young man touches the barbed wire at the Tule Lake relocation center where his parents were interned during World War II.

Many "loyal" Tule Lake internees were moved to other camps, but some insisted on staying despite the arrival of a large group of newcomers. Some of the new arrivals were pro-Japanese and potential troublemakers excluded from other camps. The rest were peaceable individuals and their families who, for reasons of confusion, disillusionment, or fear had answered "no-no" on the questionnaire. Already shaken by the internment process, they became even more traumatized in the grim environment that characterized Tule Lake.

TENSION AND DESPAIR

Despite its name, no lake softened the landscape at the Tule Lake center. Rather, the camp was set in the midst of sagebrush and rocks. Summers were hot and dry, and temperatures often dropped below freezing during winter. "All I saw for

trees were watchtowers and chimneys sticking up out of the barracks,"[98] commented one resident.

As with all camps, buildings were poorly constructed, but at Tule Lake they were overcrowded as well. Eighteen thousand people were crammed into facilities designed for sixteen thousand. Food was poor and in short supply, health care was at its worst, and the administration was unwilling to listen to requests for improvements. The atmosphere was a combination of anger and despair. When agitators staged strikes, demonstrations, and protests, they drew crowds of supporters. A report sent to Washington, D.C., stated, "Tule Lake wears a grim and belligerent face. . . . Young men frequently jeer at members of the Administrative personnel and teachers . . . some colonists have shaken their fists at the Project Director."[99]

Matters came to a head in late October 1943, when Director Dillon Myer had to resolve work stoppages and protests sparked by the accidental death of a farmworker and by director Raymond Best's insensitive behavior in the matter. Myer happened to be visiting Tule Lake, and he spent several hours in conference with a grievance committee. During the conference, several thousand internees crowded around the administration building, supporting the protest.

Three nights later, a group of angry internees attempted to stop WRA personnel from removing food from the center, claiming it was being stolen for use by Caucasian personnel. A fight broke out between camp security and the internees. In the scuffle, one staff member was hurt. Myer later described the incident as it was reported to him. "The advance of this crowd was resisted by several WRA internal security officers one of whom tripped, struck his head on a stone, and was then struck by evacuees with clubs. No other person was injured."[100]

Emotions were at a fever pitch, however, and the incident turned into a larger demonstration. Internees surged toward Director Raymond Best's residence, demanding his attention. With the crowd heading his way, Best called in army tanks and troops, which were a part of the segregation center's high security.

The center remained under military control for over two months. There were unannounced searches of residents' barracks for items such as knives and hatchets, and small groups of internees waiting to use the laundries or showers were fired on with tear gas. Lead agitators and residents who were unlucky enough to be arrested were locked into a prison within a prison called "the stockade," where sanitary conditions were primitive and food was scarce. "We were on a carrot diet from January 16 for nearly one month and [ate] carrots day after day,"[101] said one man. In the stockade, uncooperative detainees were often severely beaten. Visitors and mail were prohibited, so family members in other parts of the center had no idea what was happening to a loved one.

Within the stockade lay "the bull pen"—a high-security region reserved for the worst offenders. There, brutalized inmates slept on the ground in unheated tents even in the winter. No medical attention was given to their wounds or illnesses. One man described his time in the enclosure as "a life and death struggle for survival [in a] God Forsaken concentration camp,"[102] one he would never forget.

The stockade continued to be a part of the center, even after the military restored control to the WRA in January 1944. Appeals to the American Civil Liberties Union in mid-1944 brought help to internees confined there, however. The organization hired San Francisco attorney Wayne Collins, who threatened to go public with the abuses unless the prisoners were released by camp authorities. The stockade was demolished shortly thereafter.

OUT OF CONTROL

The WRA defended the military crackdown at Tule Lake on the basis that center residents deserved to live in a safe and

A "Riot" at Tule Lake

"Senator Albert B. Chandler (D.) of Kentucky . . . said yesterday that disloyal Jap rioters in western internment camps should be transferred to special quarters in the Aleutian Islands [off the coast of Alaska].

Chandler, who headed an investigation of the Japanese camps a year ago, warned that trouble would result from the 'coddling' of prisoners by the War Relocation Authority under Director Dillon S. Myer.

'These disloyal Japanese have no place at all in the American way of life,' Chandler said. 'I am convinced that they came here only to make trouble.

. . . 'If the Army had been put in charge of these camps, as we suggested, these recent riots would never have occurred,' Chandler continued. 'I think Mr. Myer now has a clear idea of what our committee meant when it urged the change.' Myer, head of the whole Relocation Authority, was held a prisoner in the Tule Lake camp for several hours by Jap rioters."

stable environment. That argument lacked sincerity, especially after the center's administration allowed a militant pro-Japanese group to rise to power in the camp in mid-1944. Led by angry, disillusioned transferees from other camps, the group called itself "the resegregationists" because they at first asked to be separated from other camp residents who were more pro-American in their outlook. When the administration ignored their requests, they decided to pursue a Japanese way of life within the confines of the camp. They also planned to repatriate to Japan after the war.

The resegregationists not only championed a Japanese lifestyle, but they also encouraged all residents at Tule Lake to do the same. Internees were urged—and then bullied—into enrolling in classes that taught Japanese political ideology, language, cooking, and culture. They were also pressured into learning the discipline of a "true Japanese." This included getting up early to take cold showers, taking part in strenuous militaristic drills, marching, and wearing Japanese emblems. They were instructed to speak only Japanese. More importantly, they were strongly urged to renounce their U.S. citizenship.

The "pressure boys" as some of the resegregationists were called, played on everyone's fear and bitterness in order to promote repatriation. They were also willing to use violence to make their points. One young woman wrote at the time, "It's almost as bad as being in Germany. . . . These guys have no respect for women, and boy, do they believe in Gestapo methods."[103]

ACLU director Ernest Besig, who visited the camps and noted the pro-Japanese activities, warned Director Best that it was wrong for innocent families to have to live under such conditions and wrong for parents to be forced to send their children to pro-Japanese language schools. He particularly objected to once-loyal Nisei being indoctrinated with Japanese sentiment. Besig described the director's reply. "Mr. Best told me that the maintenance of those schools was justified because 'the evacuees would be sent to Japan anyway so it was desirable to have them learn about Japanese culture.'"[104]

RENUNCIATION

The ordinarily difficult process of renunciation was made easier in 1944 by an act of Congress. Signed by president Roosevelt in July, Public Law 405 allowed citizens on American soil to renounce their citizenship during a time of war and was designed specifically for Japanese Americans. Rationale for the new law was simple: Authorities knew that several challenges to internment were in the courts and that detention of American citizens could be judged unconstitutional might soon. If that occurred, they wanted to be able to keep troublemakers locked up, and what better reason to hold them than because they had renounced their citizenship and become true "disloyals." No one paid attention to the fact that many internees would act illogically, as they ultimately did at Tule Lake.

The Supreme Court ruled against internment in December 1944. Shortly thereafter the WRA announced that camps would close. The announcement led to panic at Tule Lake. Rumors started by radicals warned that residents would soon be thrown out of camp to be killed, young men would be drafted, and families would be separated. One of the most outrageous rumors held that everyone was going to be sent back to Japan because they had voted "no-no." The U.S. government was going to report to the Japanese government anyone's unwillingness to renounce their U.S. citizenship, and reprisals would take place when residents landed.

According to the pressure boys, there was only one way to escape such a fearful fate: renunciation of citizenship. One historian writes, "By simply declaring loyalty to the Emperor and tossing off what amounted to a mere 'scrap of paper,' they could cancel out forced resettlement, rule out the draft, and extend protective custody for the entire family."[105]

MASS MOVEMENT

In the midst of the upheaval, Justice Department officials arrived to hold renunciation hearings in the camps. Dillon Myer, knowing that tensions at Tule Lake made it the worst possible time for internees to decide their future, asked the attorney general to postpone the process. His request was ignored. "Our worst fears were realized," he wrote.

> Groups of noisy, defiant young residents took to gathering at the fence . . . and demanded the right to renounce immediately. The so-called Japanese patriotic societies seized the opportunity to increase their prestige and their membership. . . . Rumors about impending government action were again rife, and these and other techniques were used as pressure on the young Nisei and Kibei to renounce their citizenship.[106]

Although in all other camps just over one hundred petitions to renounce were filed, at Tule Lake there were almost six thousand. Few who renounced citizenship realized that their requests were irreversible. "With our large family, nothing on hand, and no money to support ourselves, we have to do without food, no house to live in. So I thought it was alright to renounce it for the duration,"[107] one man explained.

TOO LATE

As numbers of renunciants grew alarmingly large, the WRA finally took action. Pro-Japanese leaders who had stirred up trouble were transferred to Justice Department internment camps. After their departure, the atmosphere at Tule Lake changed. Emotions quieted down. With time to think, many internees realized that they had made a terrible mistake. They were not loyal to Japan, and they did not want to relocate there. America was their homeland. To leave would be unthinkable.

Desperately, many sent letters to the ACLU in San Francisco asking for help. They begged it to convince the government to disregard their petitions. One man wrote, "We were under strong pressure. . . . I did not think the outcome would be so serious as to have our citizenship stripped from us. . . . You must believe me when I state that the camp pressures, rumors and built-up advice led me into this confused situation. Under normal conditions we would never think of doing what we have done."[108]

It would take more than letters to repair the harm that had been done at Tule Lake, however. One historian writes,

> Considering the background of the renunciations and the admitted injustices of the original evacuation, it would have seemed a mere matter of attempting to right a wrong for the government to cancel a renunciation upon request. Instead, for the next fourteen years the government . . . stubbornly fought every effort made through the courts to restore citizenship which it had made so very easy for the Nisei to renounce.[109]

Chapter

6 Breakthrough

By 1944 Americans were no longer afraid of a Japanese attack on the United States, but prejudice against Japanese Americans remained high in the West. Businesspeople and labor unions worried about a loss of profits if Japanese workers were allowed to return and compete with whites for jobs. Racists opposed the possible "social or sexual mixing of 'Japs' with their own pure young people"[110] and suggested that all American Japanese be sent away, perhaps to an island in the Pacific. Even many ordinary people continued to believe the worst about the Japanese. A poll taken right after the war indicated that 66 percent of respondents felt that Japanese Americans had been involved in espionage activities for the Japanese government.

POLITICAL PRACTICALITIES

Although negative attitudes remained, a greater number of people worked for increased tolerance and acceptance. Churches emphasized justice and compassion. Magazines such as the *Nation,* the *New Republic,* and the *Christian Century* published sympathetic articles about Japanese Americans. Well-known enter-

tainers such as Frank Sinatra and Bob Hope praised Japanese American military men they had visited overseas.

Two of the most influential men to speak out on behalf of Japanese Americans were Dillon Myer and Secretary of the Interior Harold Ickes. In March 1943 Myer wrote to Secretary of War Stimson

Secretary of the Interior Harold Ickes argued in June, 1944, directly to President Roosevelt for the repeal of exclusion.

LEGALIZATION OF RACISM

In a 6 to 3 decision, the Supreme Court upheld the guilty verdict against Fred Korematsu in December 1944. Some of the justices, however, were outraged that such a violation of individual rights could be tolerated. Justice Frank Murphy was one of the most plainspoken. A portion of his dissenting opinion is included in Peter Irons's book, Justice Delayed: The Record of the Japanese American Internment Cases.

"I dissent . . . from this legalization of racism. Racial discrimination in any form and in any degree has no justifiable part whatever in our democratic way of life. It is unattractive in any setting but it is utterly revolting among a free people who have embraced the principles set forth in the Constitution of the United States. All residents of this nation are kin in some way by blood or culture to a foreign land. Yet they are primarily and necessarily a part of the new and distinct civilization of the United States. They must accordingly be treated at all times as the heirs of the American experiment and as entitled to all the rights and freedoms guaranteed by the Constitution."

recommending that the order that kept the Japanese off the West Coast be relaxed. "After many months of operating relocation centers, the War Relocation Authority is convinced that they are undesirable institutions and should be removed from the American scene as soon as possible. . . . [Internment] has added weight to the contention of the enemy that . . . this nation preaches democracy and practices racial discrimination."[111] Stimson rejected Myer's recommendation, stating it was premature to consider that danger was past.

A year later, in June 1944, Ickes went straight to President Franklin Roosevelt to push for the repeal of exclusion. The WRA had been made a part of the Department of the Interior in February 1944, despite the fact that Ickes was one of the most verbal critics of internment in the president's cabinet. "The continued retention of these innocent people in the relocation centers would be a blot upon the history of this country,"[112] he stated.

The president no longer feared a Japanese attack on the West Coast. General John DeWitt had been removed from the Western Defense Command in late 1943, and his successor reported on conditions on the West Coast with a calmer perspective. Yet FDR hesitated to make any sweeping changes for fear of public criticism. The presidential election was coming up in November 1944, and he wanted to be reelected. He decided to preserve the status quo, with internees slowly leaving camps under existing WRA leave programs. He said on June 12, 1944: "The more I think of this problem of suddenly ending the orders excluding Japanese Americans from the West Coast, the more I think it would be a mistake to do anything drastic or sudden. As I said at Cabinet, I think the whole problem, for the sake of internal quiet, should be handled gradually."[113]

THE ATTITUDE OF THE COURTS

Several Japanese Americans were not willing to wait for the government to recognize and correct the injustice it had committed. Almost from the beginning they challenged internment in the courts. In their struggles, they not only battled prejudice, indifference, and the court's hesitation to question the military, but they also faced opposition from the Japanese American Citizens League. The latter opposed all legal protest because it violated its policy of total obedience to the government.

Throughout the internment years, the Supreme Court, led by Chief Justice Harlan F. Stone, was reluctant to interfere with the War Department's decision to lock up Japanese Americans, even if that decision raised constitutional questions. Most justices conformed to the accepted view that there was no easy way to determine the loyalty of Japanese Americans. Thus, curfews, evacuation, and detainment were military necessities. Judges who raised doubts about the correctness of that position were frowned on by their constituents. "The job of the Court is to resolve doubts, not create them,"[114] Stone reproved Justice Frank Murphy when he disagreed with the rest of the Court in 1943.

Associate justice of the Supreme Court Frank Murphy was reproved when he wrote that separating Japanese Americans into wartime internment camps amounted to "the legalization of racism."

Confronted with cases that involved questions of constitutional violations, the justices chose to determine each on the narrowest grounds possible. In this way, they dealt with specifics and avoided addressing the big picture—whether military necessity existed, whether the loyalty of Japanese Americans could be easily determined, and so forth. Only with the passing of time and the presentation of an open-and-shut case did they finally rule that the internment process was illegal.

THE FIRST CHALLENGERS

One of the first challengers to internment was a young attorney named Minoru Yasui. In late March 1942, convinced that his rights as an American citizen were being violated, Yasui set out to defy the 8:00 P.M.

curfew that existed for Japanese in his hometown of Portland, Oregon. He was arrested, and while awaiting trial, he was ordered to report to an assembly center in his area. He purposefully disobeyed that order, too, and had to be escorted to the center. He was then transported to Minidoka Relocation Center in Idaho, where he continued to appeal his case to higher courts.

Gordon Hirabayashi was a second Nisei who protested internment and was arrested in 1942 for violating curfew and for failing to report to an evacuation center. A Quaker and a senior at the University of Washington, Hirabayashi claimed that the government violated the Fifth Amendment by restricting the freedom of Japanese American citizens.

Both the Yasui and Hirabayashi cases went to the U.S. Supreme Court, which heard them in May 1943. Since issues in both were the same, the two were considered companion cases. On June 21, 1943, the justices ruled that the men were guilty of disobeying curfew and evacuation orders that had been created by the military for national security reasons. "The immediate responsibility for defense must necessarily rest on those who direct our armed forces," Justice Hugo Black later wrote. "Final authority to say [which] persons in the area were to be subjected to the curfew regulation was . . . not in the courts, but in the military department charged with protecting the country against pressing danger."[115]

Although Justice Frank Murphy sided with Black and the rest of the Court, issues of racism raised by the cases also concerned him. He expressed his opinion in the following statement:

Today is the first time, so far as I am aware, that we have sustained a substantial restriction of the personal liberty of citizens of the United States based upon the accident of race or ancestry. Under the curfew order here challenged no less than 70,000 American citizens have been placed under a special ban and deprived of their liberty because of their particular racial inheritance. In this sense it bears a melancholy resemblance to the treatment accorded to members of the Jewish race in Germany and in other parts of Europe.[116]

SECOND THOUGHTS

Fred Korematsu's internment challenge, when it came under scrutiny a year later, also caused certain members of the Supreme Court serious concerns. Korematsu was a young welder in the San Francisco Bay area when the order for internment was announced. Even before Pearl Harbor, he had tried twice to enlist in the army but had been turned down because of a physical disability. An obviously loyal citizen with no criminal record, he then found work in defense plants in the area.

When the evacuation order came in early 1942, Korematsu decided to ignore it since it would mean leaving his Caucasian fiancée. Intending to move out of the evacuated area with her in the near future, he passed himself off for a time as

In 1983 Fred Korematsu (left), Minoru Yasui (center), and Gordon Hirabayashi (right), filed petitions to have their cases reopened in U.S. District Court.

Chinese or Spanish Hawaiian. Soon, however, he was identified and arrested. After being tried in federal court, he was found guilty of purposely violating the Civilian Exclusion Order.

Korematsu was confined in Topaz Relocation Center in Utah while his lawyers appealed his case. That took time. Not until December 18, 1944, did Supreme Court justices deliver their opinion. By then, they were having second thoughts about the implications of imprisoning citizens indefinitely. They had had time to question the military necessity of internment. Although the case was de-

cided against Korematsu, Justice Murphy, Justice Owen J. Roberts, and Justice Robert H. Jackson dissented outright with the ruling.

Roberts stated in his opinion that Korematsu's case was not so much about excluding a person from a prohibited area. It was about the government punishing a citizen for not submitting to imprisonment in a concentration camp "based on his ancestry, and solely because of his ancestry, without evidence or inquiry concerning his loyalty and good disposition towards the United States." Roberts went on to say, "I need hardly labor the conclusion that Constitutional rights have been violated."[117]

The majority opinion, written by Justice Hugo Black, carried the day, however. He wrote,

> We uphold the exclusion order as of the time it was made and when the petitioner violated it. . . . In doing so, we are not unmindful of the hardships imposed by it upon a large group of American citizens. . . . Compulsory exclusion of large groups of citizens from their homes, except under circumstances of direst emergency and peril, is inconsistent with our basic governmental institutions. But when under conditions of modern warfare our shores are threatened by hostile forces, the power to protect must be commensurate with [equal to] the threatened danger.[118]

THE MOVE FOR LIBERATION

On June 2, 1944, Secretary of the Interior Harold Ickes wrote a letter to President Roosevelt, attempting to persuade him that internment should be brought to an immediate end. His arguments, which started the move for liberation, are included in Michi Weglyn's Years of Infamy.

"1. I have been informally advised by officials of the War Department . . . that there is no substantial justification for continuation of a ban from the standpoint of military security.

2. The continued exclusion of American citizens of Japanese ancestry from the affected areas is clearly unconstitutional in the present circumstances. . . .

3. The continuation of the exclusion orders in the West Coast areas is adversely affecting our efforts to relocate Japanese Americans elsewhere in the country. . . .

4. The psychology of the Japanese Americans in the relocation centers becomes progressively worse. The difficulty which will confront these people in readjusting to ordinary life becomes greater as they spend more time in the centers.

5. The children in the centers are exposed solely to the influence of persons of Japanese ancestry. They are becoming a hopelessly maladjusted generation, apprehensive of the outside world and divorced from the possibility of association [with]—or even seeing to any considerable extent—Americans of other races. . . .

I will not comment at this time on the justification or lack thereof for the original evacuation order. But I do say that the continued retention of these innocent people in the relocation centers would be a blot upon the history of this country."

EVACUATION COMPLICATIONS

Gordon Hirabayashi's stand against curfew and evacuation landed him in trouble with authorities in his hometown of Seattle, Washington. His trial and conviction in the U.S. district court was only the beginning of his skirmishes with the government, however. He describes his experiences during the next few months in William Petersen's Japanese Americans: Oppression and Success.

"At the U.S. District Court, I was given a sentence of 30 days for curfew violation and 30 days for refusing to evacuate, the two sentences to be served (concurrently) in the federal tank of the county jail. When I requested a sentence to the prison camp, the judge changed the sentence to three months for each charge. . . .

My case was appealed, and I remained confined in Seattle for five months in addition to the original 30 days. At the end of the fifth month a compromise arrangement was made that . . . I could be released in Spokane rather than to an evacuation camp. . . . In Spokane, I worked with the Quakers, assisting with the relocation of Japanese families. . . .

A couple of months after the Supreme Court ruled against me, the FBI looked me up and informed me that I should report to the federal tank of the Spokane County jail, to serve my sentence. When I reminded them that I was given this particular sentence in order that I might serve it in a camp, the district attorney had to be brought in for a ruling. It was ruled . . . that I could report to the nearest federal prison camp. The nearest one was located near Tacoma, which was in the excluded area; therefore my only other option was the federal prison camp near Tucson. Having given me the option, he said that I would have to get there at my own expense if I wished to go there. . . .

I decided to hitchhike. In those gas-ration days rides were not too plentiful, and it took me approximately two weeks. When I finally got to Tucson, they could not locate the papers by which I could be placed in camp. I was invited to leave, but feeling that, sooner or later, the papers would be found and I would be interrupted later on, I insisted that they find something that would allow me to begin serving my sentence, so that I could get it over with. It took several hours and, in the meantime, I roamed around Tucson without enjoying the fact that it was also an excluded area, because neither the officials nor I realized it."

EX PARTE ENDO

The fourth and final challenge to internment came from a young Nisei woman named Mitsuye Endo. Endo, a civil servant with a brother serving in the army, obeyed evacuation orders and was interned in the Tule Lake center in 1942. She was later transferred to Topaz, Utah.

With the help of a lawyer, Endo applied for a writ of habeas corpus, demanding that the courts decide the legality of her imprisonment. Endo argued that she had been cleared for indefinite leave, which signified that she was a loyal citizen, but she had not been released. She maintained that the government had no right to detain a loyal citizen who had not broken any laws.

Endo filed her petition in 1942. She waited two years for her case to come before the Supreme Court. It was decided on the same day as Fred Korematsu's, but the decision was significantly different than his had been. With *Ex Parte Endo*, as the case was called, the Court ruled on a set of circumstances that were clearly unconstitutional. Unlike Yasui, Hirabayashi, and Korematsu, Endo had not broken even the most minor law. Her challenge was not to the constitutionality of curfews or evacuations; rather, it was about imprisoning innocent citizens who had done no wrong. Justice William O. Douglas delivered the majority opinion in the case, which read, in part, "A citizen who is concededly loyal presents no problem of espionage or sabotage. Loyalty is a matter of the heart and mind, not of race, creed, or color. He who is loyal is by definition not a spy or a saboteur."[119]

Justice Roberts hammered the point home: "An admittedly loyal citizen has been deprived of her liberty for a period of years. Under the Constitution she should be free to come and go as she pleases. Instead, her liberty of motion and other innocent activities have been prohibited and conditioned. She should be discharged."[120]

Even though they condemned the imprisonment of innocent citizens, the justices did not choose to place blame of internment on those who were responsible—the military, the president, and Congress. Instead, they focused on a technicality. Executive orders authorizing evacuation had been "silent on detention," they ruled. That is, the orders had made no specific mention of holding evacuees against their will. Thus, detention, according to the Court, had not been authorized as part of the original evacuation program. Instead, the fault was with the WRA, which was guilty of exceeding its power in detaining loyal citizens.

"NOT SO GOOD"

Roosevelt was reelected in November 1944, so the conclusion of the Endo case was all the government needed to call an end to internment. On December 17, the day before the Supreme Court ruling, Roosevelt listened while the head of the Western Defense Command made the announcement:

Whereas, The present military situation makes possible . . . the termination of the system of mass exclusion of persons of Japanese ancestry . . . I, H. C. Pratt, Major General, U.S. Army, by virtue of the authority vested in me as . . . Commanding General, Western Defense Command do hereby declare and proclaim that, effective January 2, 1945. . . . Civilian Exclusion Orders . . . are rescinded.[121]

The exclusion order was officially lifted on the second day of the new year. Suddenly Japanese Americans were free to go anywhere they chose—north, south, east, or west. Ironically, like the residents of Tule Lake, many found that after three years of imprisonment, freedom was too frightening to contemplate. "I was afraid this was going to happen," an Issei said. "They said that we can go any place we like, but that's not so good. This is even worse than being evacuated."[122]

7 Return to Freedom

Internees generally reacted in three ways to the end-of-internment announcement. The "hopefuls" looked forward to the future with a certain amount of confidence since they had fit into American society before the war and were sure that they could do so again. The "desperates" were middle-aged and older Issei who felt that they were too old to rebuild their lives. They were fearful rather than angry, and they shrank from the problems they knew they would have to face outside the camps. The third group, the "resentfuls," were all those who were disillusioned and bitter about the way they had been treated by the United States. Some had become pro-Japanese during internment. Some were simply tired of being pushed around and refused to cooperate. For instance, one internee who had been considering resettlement before the announcement decided he would wait until he was "shoved through the gate"[123] before leaving camp.

REQUESTS AND RECOMMENDATIONS

Residents had endless concerns about the future—did they have to leave, where should they go, how should they get there—and they bombarded camp representatives with a multitude of questions for which they had no answers. It was soon decided that everyone's concerns should be presented to the War Relocation Authority. As a result, the All Center Conference was scheduled. Delegates from all centers except Manzanar gathered together in Salt Lake City on February 16, 1945, along with representatives from groups such as the Japanese American Citizens League, the American Civil Liberties Union, Christian and Buddhist churches, and the like. The conference ran for a week. By its end, delegates had compiled a "Statement of Facts," which ranged from assertions that "mental suffering has been caused by the forced mass evacuation" and "residents feel insecure and apprehensive towards the many changes and modifications of WRA policies" to reminders that "the residents have prepared to remain for the duration because of many statements made by the WRA that relocation centers will be maintained for the duration of the war," and "many residents were forced to dispose of their personal and real properties . . . hence have nothing to return to."[124]

Camp representatives also came up with twenty-one recommendations that they believed would help everyone make an easier transition into society. These included government low-interest loans, reinstatement of business licenses and civil-service jobs, the establishment of homes for older persons, and efforts to obtain the return of internee property. The recommendations were, according to representatives, "a statement of the minimum government assistance needed to achieve just and decent reintegration of the evacuees into American community life."[125]

The WRA ignored most of the recommendations. Internees were told they would get a one-time allowance—$25 for individuals, $50 for families—and train

THE FANATIC

When no one else would take the renunciants' cases at Tule Lake, attorney Wayne Collins stepped forward. A tireless fighter, he made their cause his top priority for over two decades. An account of his extraordinary efforts is included in The Great Betrayal: The Evacuation of the Japanese-Americans During World War II, *by Audrie Girdner and Anne Loftis.*

"When [Wayne Collins] discovered the circumstances influencing renunciation, he became indignant. The people he talked to felt themselves to be helpless pawns of fate. They doubted that anyone successfully could oppose the Army, the WRA, and the Justice Department. But in Collins they had a friend they needed, an angry man fiercely devoted to principle. Defying the government, he almost literally pulled people off the ships going to Japan. He became virtually a commuter between San Francisco; Tule Lake; Bismarck, North Dakota; Santa Fe, New Mexico; and Crystal City, Texas, in his efforts to release the renunciants and aliens and recover the citizenship of the renunciants. He made the cause of these discarded citizens his almost full-time occupation for some twenty-five years. He did not as much as take a vacation during the early years because he was fearful that something might happen to these people, who had no individual access to the United States district courts, in the event of his absence. 'I was frightened still that if I was not able to be in my office every day early and late that the government might attempt to remove all of them to Japan.' Some of his clients called him 'a brave man'; others, including Nisei, said that he was a 'fanatic' and a 'maniac.'"

fare back to the place from which they were evacuated. Army and local law enforcement officials would do their best to guard their safety during the trip, but there were no guarantees. WRA field offices in large cities would be available to help them find jobs and housing, although they could expect the offices to be overwhelmed by too many demands for help. Internees soon had to face the fact that they would be virtually on their own when their time in the camps was over.

TESTING THE WATERS

To help ease widespread fears, the WRA encouraged the most daring internees to go out into the world first. They were to "test the water," and then report back on conditions on the outside.

Their reports were valuable, but mixed. In some cases, things were better than had been expected. Churches offered to help. Neighbors had faithfully watched over possessions. Businesses could be revived. Communities were welcoming.

In many places, attitudes were changing for the better as well. Public officials recognized that opposition to returnees could have serious social and legal repercussions, and they moderated their public anti-Japanese rhetoric. For instance, Los Angeles mayor Fletcher Bowron arranged for a public ceremony for returning internees at city hall and assured them, "We want you and all other citizens of Japanese ancestry who have relocated here to feel secure in your home."[126] The new mayor of San Francisco welcomed Japan-

ese Americans who wanted to return. California governor Earl Warren announced publicly that returnees' rights must be protected and upheld. An editorial entitled "Restitution for Evacuee Citizens," which ran in a Los Angeles newspaper, showed that the conscience of at least one journalist had been pricked as well.

On the other hand, some returnees found that conditions were discouraging. Homes and farms had not been cared for or had been taken over by others. Stored furniture, household goods, and automobiles had been stolen. As the WRA reported,

> Padlocks and bolts on isolated farm buildings and deserted churches or stores afforded little protection to absentee owners against the lawless. . . . Prejudice was reflected in the indifference of many local law enforcement agencies toward the depredation [damaging] of evacuees' property and their professed inability to find or identify vandals, arsonists, and thieves.[127]

Discrimination was a continuing threat to many returnees. Agencies refused to issue licenses to those who wanted to establish businesses. Labor unions protested the hiring of Nisei in some areas. Businessmen signed agreements not to patronize Japanese establishments. The San Francisco *Chronicle* reported conditions in one region of Washington State: "Members of the anti-Nisei 'Remember Pearl Harbor' League today were on record as determined to boycott all Japanese returned to the Puyallup and White river valleys (Washington) and anyone catering to them."[128]

A Japanese American family from Seattle returned from a relocation center in Idaho in 1945 to find their home vandalized.

"NO JAPS"

One of the most negative receptions was in Hood River, Oregon, where the local American Legion post removed the names of sixteen Nisei servicemen from the town's honor roll. Signs were posted stating, "No cigarettes, No Negroes, No Japs."[129] Returnees were barred from eating in restaurants and could not buy groceries or fuel. An advertisement in the town's newspaper listed former Japanese residents and warned, "You Japs listed on this page have been told by some that you

would be welcome back in Hood River. That is not true, and this is the best time you will ever have to dispose of your property."[130]

There were no incidents of violence in Hood River, but the threat was very real both there and in other places on the West Coast in 1945. Despite assurances by the WRA that the army would protect their return, Japanese in some communities were menaced as they came into town. On farms, outbuildings were burned. Shots were fired into homes at night. One San Francisco newspaper reported, "Efforts to blow up the packing shed of a returned Japanese-American farmer with dynamite and to intimidate him and his family with gunshots were disclosed yesterday."[131] In the first half of 1945, California experienced more than thirty episodes of violence against Japanese Americans.

Returnees worked to avoid such confrontations by keeping a low profile and by tending to their own affairs. Many chose to relocate to larger cities, where people from a variety of racial backgrounds made for increased tolerance.

THE CAMPS CLOSE

Despite the dangers, internees remaining in the camps were encouraged by dozens of success stories. Families departed in groups to boost each other's courage. Trains leaving from some of the centers were full of returnees, nervous but reassured that they would not be the only ones going home. Many journeys turned into festive occasions complete with celebratory flags, banners, and singing. Returnees were also heartened by being met

RELUCTANT TO LEAVE

The announcement that internment was ending ought to have been a joyous one for camp residents. Ironically, the opposite was true, as historian Roger Daniels explains in Prisoners Without Trial: Japanese Americans in World War II.

"The policy announcement had a seemingly paradoxical result: the representatives of the inmates and the JACL officials opposed closing the camps! They felt that many of the inmates had been so impaired by their captivity and by the loss of their assets that they would not be able to live on their own.

They wanted the WRA to stay in business indefinitely and be prepared to accept responsibility for those of the exiles who, for reasons of age, infirmity, or demoralization, were not prepared to return to freedom. The inmate representatives recommended that resettlers be given financial assistance, including lump-sum grants and long-term, low-interest loans, measures that the New Deal [Roosevelt's government aid program] had instituted for all Americans during the Depression. . . . The WRA rejected all these recommendations. There would be no special aid package for the returning exiles, and those who did not leave camp voluntarily by the deadline would be given the standard relocation allowance . . . and train fare back to the place from which they had been evacuated."

at the stations by Quakers, church groups, and friends who had seen them off three years before.

Once the final exodus started, the camps closed in record time. The Jerome center in Arkansas had closed in 1944 when all of the inmates were transferred to other camps; in October 1945 Granada, Minidoka, and Topaz were shut down. Of course, some internees continued to resist the inevitable. A few people committed suicide rather than leave, and some had to be physically carried to the trains. By the end of November, however, all but Tule Lake were empty, a testament to Dillon Myer's determination that the internees should return to the world as quickly as possible.

CHANGES

Not all internees went back to the West Coast when given the chance. About fifty thousand had already relocated eastward and were putting down roots in Denver, Salt Lake City, Chicago, and other points in the Midwest and the East. As the camps closed, these were joined by family members and by others who were willing to take a chance in a new part of the country.

Relocatees who went eastward discovered—just as students had done earlier—that the move was good for them. Living in different parts of the country exposed them to different ways of thinking and broadened their outlook. Prejudice was less, so job opportunities were better. They were seen by others as individuals rather than as members of a "foreign" community, and they were judged on their merits rather than on their Japanese heritage.

Those who returned to the West Coast discovered that life had changed there in the three years that they had been away. Thousands of Americans from other states had moved to California to work in defense industries during the war. Land was owned by refugees from the Dust Bowl—Oklahoma and Texas. Former Japanese neighborhoods had become predominately African American.

Even Japanese communities, as they reestablished themselves, were different than before. The Nisei still concentrated on traditional pursuits such as family, work, church, and school. Hard work was the watchword of most. Students went back to school. Young couples set up their homes and began rearing their children. But during internment the Nisei had assumed leadership for their families and their barrack-communities, and now they retained that leadership in the outside world. The Issei—particularly older men—were left relatively powerless, deprived of the important role they had once occupied. To their shame, many were also too old to find new jobs or to learn new skills, and they thus remained unemployed. One returnee wrote, "To me the saddest thing that happened was when my father came out of internment. . . . He had to resettle in Chicago and he didn't have any money. No capital. No nothing, and even with his education. As you can imagine, a sixty-year-old man trying to get a white collar job—there was nothing available for him."[132]

MAKING DO

One of the most frustrating situations that all returnees faced was finding a place to live. Discrimination and postwar shortages made housing extremely tight. One woman remembered, "We could not get housing. . . . We have walked miles and miles every day, dragging [our daughter] Linda here and there, snatching a few hours for a nap here, carrying her there, looking for a place to stay."[133]

Internees were not too proud to take advantage of any opportunities they found, however. Many crowded together in small low-rent apartments and hostels. Some lived in cheap trailer parks. One Nisei wrote, "I came back to Los Angeles after my father and stayed at his hotel room in the skid row area. There was only one room, and only one bed, he worked the graveyard shift and I went to school during the day, therefore, we managed to use the same bed at different hours of the day."[134]

For the most desperate, church and community groups provided temporary housing, as did the federal government's National Housing Agency and Public Housing Administration. As the war ended, empty military barracks were also called into use. Even the WRA provided blankets, cots, tents, and cooking utensils when no other aid was available.

Jobs were almost as hard to find as housing. Some internees discovered that their businesses had survived, but most had to start again with little or no money. Competition was fierce, and most took any job they could find. Single men and women felt lucky if they could get gar-

dening or housekeeping positions since room and board was often provided. Professionals made do with manual labor. Men who wanted to get back into farming worked as hired hands. Some found that industries such as fish canneries were willing to hire Japanese Americans. Others started small restaurants, repair shops, and the like.

RIGHTING LEGAL WRONGS

Internees endured great mental suffering, hardship, and loss caused by internment, but they were slow to turn to the courts for restitution. There were exceptional cases, however. For instance, in response to the state of California seizing over a quarter of a million dollars' worth of property from landowning Issei during internment, even the conservative JACL decided that steps needed to be taken to defend property rights. Aided by ACLU attorneys, men like Fred Oyama, who had initially lost his bid to keep land given to him by his Issei father, took his case as far as the Supreme Court. There, he won after the Court found that his rights as a citizen had been violated.

Such actions gave the courts opportunities to rule against discriminatory laws. In 1948 Oregon's supreme court struck down the state's Alien Land Law. In 1950 a California district court of appeals decided that the California version was also unenforceable.

In 1952 Congress passed the McCarran-Walter Immigration and Naturalization Act, which had the strong support of the

JACL. The bill not only allowed for limited immigration from Japan each year, it also allowed Japanese aliens to become naturalized U.S. citizens. About twenty thousand Issei rushed to become citizens between 1952 and 1957. One man commented that taking the oath of citizenship was "the greatest happiness and fortune we have ever received in our lifetime."[135]

THE EVACUATION CLAIMS ACT

In another attempt to right widespread legal wrongs, in 1946 the JACL asked Congress to compensate evacuees for physical losses caused by internment. Unfortunately, no one had kept an exact tally of each family's losses. The evacuees themselves had been too upset and too rushed to make exact appraisals of all of the goods they sold, gave away, or lost. Tax records that would have been

informative had been destroyed. The JACL could only estimate that property losses totaled approximately $400 million in 1942 values.

Despite the obstacles, the JACL request had the strong support of Secretary of the Interior Harold Ickes and J. A. Krug (Ickes's successor). Both men supported an evacuation claims bill, and President Harry Truman expressed his willingness to sign one should it be placed before him. In 1948 the Evacuation Claims Act became law, authorizing the attorney general to judge claims filed as a result of internment. The law was extremely limited, however. Claimants had only eighteen months to file and could not include losses in earned income and earning power or losses relating to personal injury, personal inconvenience, physical hardship, mental suffering, or death. The government set aside only $38 million to cover the claims, and no one could receive more than $2,500.

Hundreds of Issei took the final oath of citizenship in Washington, D.C., in 1954.

Almost twenty-seven thousand claims totaling $148 million were filed under the act. Under intense government scrutiny, however, many claims were rejected on the basis of technicalities. For instance, in the case of Yasuhei Nagashima,

> [He] received $308.75 for goods stored with the WRA and erroneously sold at public auction. However, a claim for a loss of $499 incurred in the sale of his truck was not allowed; the claimant, in ignorance of the law, had not originally included this item, and an amendment to his claim that introduced new subject matter constituted "an insurmountable bar" to settlement.[136]

The average award per claimant was about $440, and due to the slowness of the process, many older internees died before their cases were reviewed. A total of $36 million in claims was eventually paid, "which of course did not cover all the losses,"[137] Dillon Myer noted with regret.

THE FIGHT AGAINST DEPORTATION

As the majority of internees dealt with the burden of reestablishing their homes, finding jobs, and fitting back into society, a minority were confronted with a different kind of ordeal. Tule Lake residents who had rashly renounced their citizenship during the turbulent days of 1944 faced the consequences of their decisions. They were without rights and were going to be deported to Japan, whether or not they

still wanted to go. Many of their number had appealed for help to the ACLU, but no lawyer seemed willing to take their case.

Then attorney Wayne Collins stepped forward again. A strong believer in civil rights, he could not stand by while helpless citizens were in trouble. "Renunciation was not the product of free will but was forced upon them by the unlawful detention and the conditions prevailing at the Tule Lake Center, *for which the government alone was responsible*. In consequence every renunciation was the direct product of government duress,"[138] he insisted.

In November 1945 Collins filed suits in federal court asking that his clients—987 persons—be released and their renunciations voided. He based his petitions on the fact that all had been pressured to make their decisions while being unconstitutionally held in camp. The suits alleged that the government had condoned the pressure by failing to segregate loyal internees from those who were pressuring them.

Collins's proceedings halted the expulsion of some renunciants to Japan, and the Justice Department agreed to release most individuals under the age of twenty-one. It also agreed to hold further hearings in the matter, although petitioners needed to show "just cause" for why they should not be deported. Over 3,000 people decided to petition. As a result of these hearings, which began in January 1946, all but 449 "rejectees" were allowed to remain in the United States. The balance joined other individuals who, for various reasons, wanted to leave. According to one historian, "Some eight thousand persons of Japanese descent (including repatriates and expatriates from other camps) left for Japan between V-J Day [August 15] and mid-1946."[139]

THE CLOSE OF "AN INFAMOUS CHAPTER"

Once he had saved most of his clients from being deported, Collins continued the fight to restore their citizenship. It was a long battle. On March 23, 1949, he believed he had won when U.S. District Court Judge Louis E. Goodman declared the renunciations unconstitutional and restored citizenship to Collins's clients, who now numbered some five thousand Nisei. The government appealed Goodman's decision, however. Then, in 1950, the Ninth Circuit Court of Appeals in San Francisco decided that Collins had to prove individually that each renunciant had made a decision while under pressure.

Collins fought back. As he later remembered,

> I informed [the attorney general] and his agents that it would take me considerably over thirty years, or, if I engaged the services of other lawyers to assist me it would take up some ten years of constant trial and would tie up the three federal judges in San Francisco to the exclusion of any other cases since my cases would have priority in trial dates.[140]

The warning was heeded, and Collins was told that each renunciant had only to supply a sworn statement explaining why he or she had renounced.

San Francisco attorney Wayne Collins labored to restore the rights of Japanese Americans until 1968, when the last case was resolved.

Nine years passed while everyone waited and hoped. Finally, in May 1959, the government announced that its review of the renunciation cases was complete and that citizenship had been restored to 4,978 Nisei. It was a significant victory, although Collins continued to fight a few exceptionally complicated cases. Not until 1968 was the battle finally over.

When it was, Collins looked back on the long struggle with a feeling of justifiable triumph. "The fundamental rights, liberties, privileges and immunities of these citizens are now honored," he said. "The discrimination practiced against them by the government has ceased. The episode which constituted an infamous chapter in our history has come to a close."[141]

Final Justice

As decades passed, America tried to forget the internment episode, particularly as more people came to see it as a racially motivated and very expensive mistake. (The War Department estimated in the 1940s that the cost of evacuation, construction of assembly and relocation centers, and support for the War Relocation Authority totaled over $400 million. Economic losses as a result of thousands of adults being taken from the workforce totaled an additional $70 million.) The episode was not mentioned in textbooks or in encyclopedias. No monuments marked the camps or memorialized the centers. Statesmen like Franklin D. Roosevelt and Earl Warren were remembered for their support of human freedoms, not for their contribution to racial injustice.

Japanese Americans did not speak of their internment experience either, not even to their children. One Nisei writer explained: "The government we trusted had betrayed us. Acknowledging such a reality was so difficult that our natural feelings of rage, fear, and helplessness were turned inward and buried. . . . We were ashamed and humiliated."[142]

In 1987 current Secretary of Transportation Norman Mineta revisited his parents' home in San Jose, California. He and his family were evacuated from this house in 1942.

Despite their traumatic experience, however, the majority remained law abiding, unassuming, and eager to blend into their communities. Quietly, they established themselves in mainstream society and became known as "the model minority" as they achieved middle-class status, attained a higher level of education than did the general population, and gradually filled positions in education, medicine, law, and business that had been closed to them in earlier decades.

SPEAKING OUT

The children of the Nisei, dubbed the Sansei, were too young to suffer lingering effects of the internment experience. Most had not been born in the 1940s. As they grew older, they were comfortable with their heritage, confident of their rights as Americans, and more assertive than their parents. Although they were inclined to blend into American society, they did not hesitate to speak out against injustice.

When the Sansei learned about their parents' years behind barbed wire, they were angry, both at the government that had carried out the injustice and at their parents because they had submitted to internment without a struggle. Why had the Japanese American community let such an offense take place, they wondered. Why hadn't someone put up a fight? "We would argue," says one young man. "I couldn't understand why they just packed up and went without resistance."[143]

As the questions of the younger generation set them thinking, many Nisei decided that hiding their feelings was leading to bitterness. They needed to speak out about their experiences. Some began writing and published accounts of the episode. Some made pilgrimages to now-deserted camps. Some merely talked openly to family and friends about their internment memories.

With the talking came a measure of relief and healing. "You talk to people and they start sitting down and tears start trickling down their cheeks—that's how important that thing was,"[144] says one of the younger generation. As they expressed their feelings about internment, most internees realized that they had done nothing to deserve their ill treatment. In fact, they had been almost too accommodating. They also realized that a great injustice had been done to them as American citizens, and that some sort of redress or restitution needed to be made before they could permanently put the experience behind them.

THE REDRESS MOVEMENT

During the 1970s both the JACL and the newly formed National Council for Japanese American Redress began movements to get compensation for wrongs done to Japanese Americans during internment. Their justification for asking the government to make amends was simple and straightforward. As a JACL redress committee pamphlet explained, "Restitution does not put a price tag on freedom or justice. The issue is not to recover what cannot be recovered. The issue is to acknowledge the mistake by providing proper redress to victims of injustice and thereby make such injustices less likely to recur."[145] Chief Justice William Denman of the Ninth Circuit Court of Appeals stated it more succinctly: "When wrongs are deliberately committed upon its citizens by a civilized nation, ordinary decent standards require that compensation be made."[146]

Not every Japanese American supported the move for redress. Some saw it as a demand for welfare. Some saw it as a futile effort. A chief opponent was S. I. Hayakawa, who had been elected to the U.S. Senate in 1976. He stated a widely held opinion that relocation had actually been good for the Japanese. "As many [Nisei] say, the relocation forced them out of their segregated existence to discover the rest of America. It opened up possibilities for them that they never would have known had they remained on farms in Livingston or fishing boats in San Pedro."[147] Supporters of restitution pointed out irately that Hayakawa had been in Chicago during the internment years and therefore could not speak from personal experience.

Acknowledging "a Grave Injustice"

Despite objections from some, the movement gained momentum as time passed.

Visiting the ruins of Tule Lake and other relocation centers has helped heal the wounds of internment for many detainees, their children, and grandchildren.

It was aided by Congress in 1980 with the formation of the Commission on the Wartime Relocation and Internment of Civilians. The commission was a nine-member multiethnic body made up of former members of Congress, Supreme Court justices, and respected civic leaders. In the course of its investigations it interviewed more than seven hundred people (many of them internees) and reviewed internment-related documents. Its report, *Personal Justice Denied*, laid bare the truth about internment, including the discriminatory attitudes of those who pushed for it, the lack of military necessity for evacuating the West Coast, and the suffering endured by the Japanese American community. "A grave injustice was done to American citizens and resident aliens of Japanese ancestry who, without individual review or any probative [factual] evidence against them, were excluded, removed and detained by the United States during World War II."[148]

The commission recommended that Congress publicly acknowledge and apologize for wrongs done to the Japanese American community and that restitution in the amount of $20,000 be given to each of the survivors of internment. An estimated sixty thousand internees were still alive at that time, so the total cost would be $1.2 billion. In 1988 Congress passed legislation supporting such redress, and in October 1990 the first checks—accompanied by a letter of apology signed by President George Bush—were put in the mail. Justice had been long in coming, but official recognition went far to aid the healing.

At about the same time that the commission was wrapping up its findings, Minoru Yasui, Gordon Hirabayashi, and Fred Korematsu went to court asking that federal judges reverse their convictions. They based their arguments on the discovery in 1981 by author Peter Irons that government lawyers and officials had withheld crucial evidence in the men's original trials. At the conclusion of the new hearings the convictions were reversed. Again, justice had been delayed, but in the end, past wrongs were righted.

CONSTANT CAUTION

Japanese American internment was a bleak time in U.S. history. Statesmen, journalists, and military men allowed racism to rule their decision making. The public enthusiastically supported such biased acts. The Supreme Court judged those actions constitutionally justifiable.

The event has merit only if it serves as a warning to future generations. In the words of federal district judge Marilyn Hall Patel, who delivered the decision in the 1983 Korematsu case,

> As historical precedent it stands as a constant caution that in times of war or declared military necessity our institutions must be vigilant in protecting constitutional guarantees. . . . It stands as a caution that in times of international hostility and antagonisms our institutions, legislative, executive, and judicial, must be pre-

KEEPING HISTORY ALIVE

Yoshiko Uchida was only a teen when she and her family were interned at the Topaz center in Utah during the war. After her release, she became an award-winning author. In her memoir Desert Exile, *she explains her desire to keep the memory of the camps alive for young Americans of every generation.*

"The wartime evacuation of the Japanese Americans has already been well documented in many fine scholarly books. . . . Still, there are many young Americans who have never heard about the evacuation. . . . As a writer of books for young people, I often speak at schools about my experiences as a Japanese American. I want the children to perceive me not as a foreigner, as some still do, or as a stereotypic Asian they often see on film and television, but as a human being. I tell them of my pride in being a Japanese American today, but I also tell them I celebrate our common humanity, for I feel we must never lose our sense of connection with the human race. I tell them how it was to grow up as a Japanese American in California. I tell them about the Issei who persevered in a land that denied them so much. I tell them how our own country incarcerated us—its citizens—during World War II, causing us to lose that most precious of all possessions, our freedom.

The children ask me many questions, most of them about my wartime experiences. 'I never knew we had concentration camps in America,' one child told me in astonishment. 'I thought they were only in Germany and Russia.'

And so the story of the wartime incarceration of the Japanese Americans, as painful as it may be to hear, needs to be told and retold and never forgotten by succeeding generations of Americans."

pared to exercise their authority to protect all citizens from the petty fears and prejudices that are so easily aroused.[149]

Internment violated the spirit of the Constitution. It laid bare the ugly strain of racism that runs through the American character. It stands as a warning that liberty is always more important than convenience or practicality, and that the rights of the few must never be recklessly sacrificed for the good of many.

Notes

Introduction: Americans Betrayed

1. Roger Daniels, *Prisoners Without Trial: Japanese Americans in World War II*. New York: Hill and Wang, 1993, p. 107.

2. Quoted in Page Smith, *Democracy on Trial*. New York: Simon and Schuster, 1995, p. 124.

3. Quoted in Peter Irons, ed., *Justice Delayed: The Record of the Japanese American Internment Cases*. Middletown, CT: Wesleyan University Press, 1989, p. 83.

4. Roger Daniels, *Concentration Camps, U.S.A.: Japanese Americans and World War II*. New York: Holt, Rinehart and Winston, 1972, p. 80.

5. John Tateishi, ed., *And Justice for All: An Oral History of the Japanese American Detention Camps*. New York: Random House, 1984, p. vii.

Chapter 1: The Japanese "Problem"

6. Audrie Girdner and Anne Loftis, *The Great Betrayal: The Evacuation of the Japanese-Americans During World War II*. New York: Macmillan, 1969, p. 33.

7. Girdner and Loftis, *The Great Betrayal*, p. 34.

8. Chinese Exclusion Act, 47th Cong., session 1, 1882. www.itp.berkeley.edu/~asam121/1882.html.

9. Quoted in Smith, *Democracy on Trial*, p. 55.

10. Quoted in Daniels, *Concentration Camps, U.S.A.*, pp. 7–8.

11. Quoted in Girdner and Loftis, *The Great Betrayal*, p. 89.

12. Quoted in Daniels, *Prisoners Without Trial*, pp. 9–10.

13. Quoted in Daniels, *Concentration Camps, U.S.A.*, p. 11.

14. Quoted in Commission on the Wartime Relocation and Internment of Civilians, *Personal Justice Denied*. Washington, DC: GPO, 1982, p. 34.

15. Yoshiko Uchida, *Desert Exile*. Seattle: University of Washington Press, 1982, p. 42.

16. Quoted in Girdner and Loftis, *The Great Betrayal*, p. 77.

17. Uchida, *Desert Exile*, p. 42.

18. Quoted in Tateishi, *And Justice for All*, p. 169.

19. Quoted in Daniels, *Prisoners Without Trial*, pp. 20–21.

20. Quoted in Girdner and Loftis, *The Great Betrayal*, p. 95.

21. Quoted in Girdner and Loftis, *The Great Betrayal*, p. 76.

22. Quoted in Girdner and Loftis, *The Great Betrayal*, p. 76.

Chapter 2: Definite Menace

23. Quoted in Girdner and Loftis, *The Great Betrayal*, p. 2.

24. Quoted in Daniels, *Concentration Camps, U.S.A.*, p. 41.

25. Jeanne Wakatsuki Houston and James D. Houston, *Farewell to Manzanar*. Boston: Houghton Mifflin, 1973, p. 7.

26. Quoted in Daniels, *Prisoners Without Trial*, p. 25.

27. Quoted in Michi Weglyn, *Years of Infamy*. New York: William Morrow, Quill Paperbacks, 1976, p. 45.

28. Quoted in Anne Reeploeg Fisher, *Exile of a Race*. Seattle: F. & T., 1965, p. 37.

29. Quoted in Dorothy Swaine Thomas and Richard S. Nishimoto, *The Spoilage.* Berkeley and Los Angeles: University of California Press, 1946, pp. 18–19.

30. Quoted in John Armor and Peter Wright, *Manzanar.* New York: Times Books, 1988, p. 38.

31. Quoted in Daniels, *Concentration Camps, U.S.A.,* p. 61.

32. Quoted in Girdner and Loftis, *The Great Betrayal,* p. 27.

33. Quoted in Daniels, *Concentration Camps, U.S.A.,* pp. 45–46.

34. Quoted in Daniels, *Prisoners Without Trial,* pp. 39–40.

35. Quoted in Armor and Wright, *Manzanar,* p. 22.

36. Quoted in Fisher, *Exile of a Race,* p. 58.

37. Quoted in Daniels, *Concentration Camps, U.S.A.,* p. 70.

38. Quoted in Dillon S. Myer, *Uprooted Americans: The Japanese Americans and the War Relocation Authority.* Tucson: University of Arizona Press, 1971, pp. 307–8.

39. Quoted in Commission on the Wartime Relocation and Internment of Civilians, *Personal Justice Denied,* p. 113.

40. Quoted in Girdner and Loftis, *The Great Betrayal,* p. 201.

41. Quoted in Girdner and Loftis, *The Great Betrayal,* p. 201.

42. Quoted in Smith, *Democracy on Trial,* p. 127.

43. Quoted in Thomas and Nishimoto, *The Spoilage,* p. 21.

44. Quoted in Weglyn, *Years of Infamy,* p. 122.

45. Quoted in Girdner and Loftis, *The Great Betrayal,* pp. 102–3.

46. Quoted in Girdner and Loftis, *The Great Betrayal,* p. 127.

47. Quoted in Smith, *Democracy on Trial,* p. 130.

Chapter 3: Military Necessity

48. Quoted in Girdner and Loftis, *The Great Betrayal,* p. 116.

49. Quoted in Richard Drinnon, *Keeper of Concentration Camps: Dillon S. Myer and American Racism.* Berkeley and Los Angeles: University of California Press, 1987, p. 3.

50. Quoted in Girdner and Loftis, *The Great Betrayal,* p. 134.

51. Quoted in Armor and Wright, *Manzanar,* p. 4.

52. Quoted in Commission on the Wartime Relocation and Internment of Civilians, *Personal Justice Denied,* p. 132.

53. Quoted in Girdner and Loftis, *The Great Betrayal,* p. 129.

54. Quoted in Girdner and Loftis, *The Great Betrayal,* pp. 132–3.

55. Quoted in Daniels, *Concentration Camps, U.S.A.,* p. 87.

56. Quoted in Girdner and Loftis, *The Great Betrayal,* p. 138.

57. Quoted in Tateishi, *And Justice for All,* p. 102.

58. Girdner and Loftis, *The Great Betrayal,* p. 147.

59. John Modell, ed., *The Kikuchi Diary.* Urbana: University of Illinois Press, 1973, p. 64.

60. Quoted in Girdner and Loftis, *The Great Betrayal,* p. 154.

61. Quoted in Girdner and Loftis, *The Great Betrayal,* p. 148.

62. Quoted in Girdner and Loftis, *The Great Betrayal,* p. 177.

63. Quoted in Daniels, *Concentration Camps, U.S.A.,* p. 89.

64. Quoted in Daniels, *Concentration Camps, U.S.A.,* p. 89.

65. Fisher, *Exile of a Race*, p. 126.

66. Quoted in Girdner and Loftis, *The Great Betrayal*, p. 173.

67. Quoted in Modell, *The Kikuchi Diary*, p. 199.

Chapter 4: Behind Barbed Wire

68. Quoted in Girdner and Loftis, *The Great Betrayal*, p. 215.

69. Quoted in Myer, *Uprooted Americans*, pp. 37–38.

70. Houston and Houston, *Farewell to Manzanar*, p. 17.

71. Quoted in Girdner and Loftis, *The Great Betrayal*, p. 234.

72. Quoted in Girdner and Loftis, *The Great Betrayal*, p. 299.

73. Quoted in Tateishi, *And Justice for All*, p. 150.

74. Quoted in Smith, *Democracy on Trial*, p. 204.

75. Quoted in Girdner and Loftis, *The Great Betrayal*, p. 305.

76. Weglyn, *Years of Infamy*, p. 105.

77. Myer, *Uprooted Americans*, p. 52.

78. Quoted in Commission on the Wartime Relocation and Internment of Civilians, *Personal Justice Denied*, p. 176.

79. Quoted in Daniels, *Concentration Camps, U.S.A.*, p. 119.

80. Girdner and Loftis, *The Great Betrayal*, p. 247.

81. Quoted in Smith, *Democracy on Trial*, p. 259.

82. Quoted in Roger Daniels, Sandra C. Taylor, and Harry H. L. Kitano, eds., *Japanese Americans: From Relocation to Redress*. Seattle: University of Washington Press, 1986, p. 88.

83. Myer, *Uprooted Americans*, p. xiv.

Chapter 5: A Question of Loyalty

84. Myer, *Uprooted Americans*, p. xiv.

85. Girdner and Loftis, *The Great Betrayal*, p. 344.

86. Quoted in Commission on the Wartime Relocation and Internment of Civilians, *Personal Justice Denied*, p. 180.

87. Quoted in Commission on the Wartime Relocation and Internment of Civilians, *Personal Justice Denied*, p. 182.

88. Quoted in Smith, *Democracy on Trial*, p. 233.

89. Quoted in Commission on the Wartime Relocation and Internment of Civilians, *Personal Justice Denied*, p. 253.

90. Quoted in Commission on the Wartime Relocation and Internment of Civilians, *Personal Justice Denied*, p. 191.

91. Quoted in Myer, *Uprooted Americans*, p. 73.

92. Quoted in Daniels, *Concentration Camps, U.S.A.*, p. 128.

93. Myer, *Uprooted Americans*, p. 146.

94. Quoted in Myer, *Uprooted Americans*, p. 149.

95. Quoted in Commission on the Wartime Relocation and Internment of Civilians, *Personal Justice Denied*, p. 184.

96. Quoted in Myer, *Uprooted Americans*, p. 72.

97. Quoted in Commission on the Wartime Relocation and Internment of Civilians, *Personal Justice Denied*, p. 196.

98. Quoted in Girdner and Loftis, *The Great Betrayal*, p. 218.

99. Quoted in Weglyn, *Years of Infamy*, p. 149.

100. Quoted in Weglyn, *Years of Infamy*, p. 163.

101. Quoted in Thomas and Nishimoto, *The Spoilage*, p. 284.

102. Quoted in Commission on the Wartime Relocation and Internment of Civilians, *Personal Justice Denied*, p. 247.

103. Quoted in Smith, *Democracy on Trial*, p. 327.

104. Quoted in Weglyn, *Years of Infamy*, pp. 213–14.

105. Weglyn, *Years of Infamy*, p. 236.

106. Myer, *Uprooted Americans*, p. 89.

107. Quoted in Thomas and Nishimoto, *The Spoilage*, p. 349.

108. Quoted in Thomas and Nishimoto, *The Spoilage*, pp. 351–52.

109. Fisher, *Exile of a Race*, p. 229.

Chapter 6: Breakthrough

110. Quoted in Girdner and Loftis, *The Great Betrayal*, p. 357.

111. Myer, *Uprooted Americans*, p. 158.

112. Quoted in Commission on the Wartime Relocation and Internment of Civilians, *Personal Justice Denied*, p. 228.

113. Quoted in Commission on the Wartime Relocation and Internment of Civilians, *Personal Justice Denied*, p. 229.

114. Quoted in Daniels, Taylor, and Kitano, *Japanese Americans*, p. 184.

115. Quoted in Daniels, Taylor, and Kitano, *Japanese Americans*, p. 176.

116. Quoted in Irons, *Justice Delayed*, p. 69.

117. Quoted in Irons, *Justice Delayed*, p. 84.

118. Quoted in Irons, *Justice Delayed*, pp. 79–80.

119. Quoted in *Ex Parte Mitsuye Endo*, December 18, 1944. http://history.wisc.edu/archdeacon/404tja/endo.html.

120. Quoted in *Ex Parte Mitsuye Endo*, December 18, 1944. http://history.wisc.edu/archdeacon/404tja/endo.html.

121. Henry C. Pratt, "Public Proclamation No. 21," Western Defense Command, U.S. Army, December 17, 1944. www.du.edu/~amballar/PP_21.html.

122. Quoted in Smith, Democracy on Trial, p. 372.

Chapter 7: Return to Freedom

123. Quoted in Smith, *Democracy on Trial*, p. 373.

124. Quoted in Smith, *Democracy on Trial*, pp. 376–77.

125. Quoted in Smith, *Democracy on Trial*, p. 380.

126. Quoted in Daniels, *Concentration Camps, U.S.A.*, p. 159.

127. Quoted in Smith, *Democracy on Trial*, p. 417.

128. Quoted in Thomas and Nishimoto, *The Spoilage*, p. 346.

129. Quoted in Girdner and Loftis, *The Great Betrayal*, p. 396.

130. Quoted in Girdner and Loftis, *The Great Betrayal*, p. 397.

131. Quoted in Thomas and Nishimoto, *The Spoilage*, p. 347.

132. Quoted in Tateishi, *And Justice for All*, p. 240.

133. Quoted in Commission on the Wartime Relocation and Internment of Civilians, *Personal Justice Denied*, pp. 204–5.

134. Quoted in Commission on the Wartime Relocation and Internment of Civilians, Personal Justice Denied, pp. 241–2.

135. Quoted in Smith, *Democracy on Trial*, p. 443.

136. Quoted in William Petersen, *Japanese Americans: Oppression and Success*. New York: Random House, 1971, p. 106.

137. Quoted in Smith, *Democracy on Trial*, p. 418.

138. Quoted in Weglyn, *Years of Infamy*, p. 256.

139. Quoted in Weglyn, *Years of Infamy*, p. 260.

140. Quoted in Weglyn, *Years of Infamy*, p. 262.

141. Quoted in Weglyn, *Years of Infamy*, p. 265.

Epilogue: Final Justice

142. Quoted in Daniels, Taylor, and Kitano, *Japanese Americans*, p. 160.

143. Quoted in Weglyn, *Years of Infamy*, p. 280.

144. Quoted in Weglyn, *Years of Infamy*, p. 281.

145. Quoted in Daniels, Taylor, and Kitano, *Japanese Americans*, p. 189.

146. Quoted in Fisher, *Exile of a Race*, p. 237.

147. Quoted in Daniels, Taylor, and Kitano, *Japanese Americans*, p. 189.

148. Quoted in Daniels, *Prisoners Without Trial*, pp. 3–4.

149. Quoted in Daniels, *Prisoners Without Trial*, p. 100.

For Further Reading

Michael Cooper, *Fighting for Honor: Japanese Americans and World War II.* New York: Clarion Books, 2000. An account of the combat experiences of Japanese Americans during World War II.

Brian J. Grapes, ed., *Japanese American Internment Camps.* San Diego: Greenhaven, 2001. A collection of essays, speeches, and firsthand accounts of internment.

Ellen Levine, *A Fence away from Freedom: Japanese Americans and World War II.* New York: G. P. Putman, 1995. This book offers personal experiences of Japanese Americans during World War II.

Diane Yancey, *Life in a Japanese American Internment Camp.* San Diego: Lucent Books, 1998. An examination of life in the assembly and relocation centers.

Works Consulted

Books

John Armor and Peter Wright, *Manzanar.* New York: Times Books, 1988. The story of internment with emphasis on Manzanar Relocation Center. Illustrated with photographs of the center and its residents by renowned photographer Ansel Adams.

Commission on the Wartime Relocation and Internment of Civilians, *Personal Justice Denied.* Washington: GPO, 1982. The definitive government report on the internment of the Japanese, published almost forty years after the fact.

Roger Daniels, *Concentration Camps, U.S.A.: Japanese Americans and World War II.* New York: Holt, Rinehart and Winston, 1972. An expert on Japanese American internment focuses on the political aspects of the episode.

———, *Prisoners Without Trial: Japanese Americans in World War II.* New York: Hill and Wang, 1993. A brief, well-written account of the Japanese in America with emphasis on their internment experiences.

Roger Daniels, Sandra C. Taylor, Harry H. L. Kitano, eds., *Japanese Americans: From Relocation to Redress.* Seattle: University of Washington Press, 1986. A selection of articles ranging from a discussion of the evacuation order to the debate over reparations in the 1970s.

Richard Drinnon, *Keeper of Concentration Camps: Dillon S. Myer and American Racism.* Berkeley and Los Angeles: University of California Press, 1987. A biography of national WRA director Dillon Myer.

Anne Reeploeg Fisher, *Exile of a Race.* Seattle: F. & T., 1965. The history of Japanese American internment, including excerpts from newspapers, magazines, and congressional hearings.

Audrie Girdner and Anne Loftis, *The Great Betrayal: The Evacuation of the Japanese-Americans During World War II.* New York: Macmillan, 1969. A lengthy and complete account of Japanese American internment; includes numerous quotes and first-person accounts.

Jeanne Wakatsuki Houston and James D. Houston, *Farewell to Manzanar.* Boston: Houghton Mifflin, 1973. The story of the Wakatsuki family's internment as told by the youngest daughter.

Peter Irons, *Justice at War: The Story of the Japanese American Internment Cases.* New York: Oxford University Press, 1983. The author reveals the government's successful efforts during the 1940s to suppress evidence that would have proven internment unnecessary.

Peter Irons, ed., *Justice Delayed: The Record of the Japanese American In-*

ternment Cases. Middletown, CT: Wesleyan University Press, 1989. Minoru Yasui, Gordon Hirabayashi, and Fred Korematsu's fight to reverse their wartime convictions, based on newly uncovered evidence of the government's suppression of key documents; includes the full text of the original Supreme Court cases.

Daisuke Kitagawa, Issei and Nisei: The Internment Years. New York: Seabury, 1967. An account of Japanese American internment, told by an internee chaplain.

John Modell, ed., The Kikuchi Diary. Urbana: University of Illinois Press, 1973. Excerpts from the journal of college student Charles Kikuchi, beginning with Pearl Harbor and continuing through his months of internment at the Tanforan Assembly Center in California.

Dillon S. Myer, Uprooted Americans: The Japanese Americans and the War Relocation Authority. Tucson: University of Arizona Press, 1971. A subjective overview of internment written by the director of the WRA.

William Petersen, Japanese Americans: Oppression and Success. New York: Random House, 1971. A comprehensive history of Japanese Americans, who they are, why they came to the United States, what they suffered there, and how they eventually succeeded.

Page Smith, Democracy on Trial. New York: Simon and Schuster, 1995. A detailed and well-written account of internment.

John Tateishi, ed., And Justice for All: An Oral History of the Japanese American Detention Camps. New York: Random House, 1984. A collection of narratives written by former internees, including Minoru Yasui and Mitsuye Endo.

Dorothy Swaine Thomas, The Salvage. Berkeley and Los Angeles: University of California Press, 1952. This book focuses on Japanese American migration from the WRA camps to the Midwest and East during 1943 and 1944 and includes life histories of fifteen resettlers. It was researched and written by social scientist Dorothy Swaine Thomas as part of a University of California study.

Dorothy Swaine Thomas and Richard S. Nishimoto, The Spoilage. Berkeley and Los Angeles: University of California Press, 1946. This book focuses on the experiences of those Japanese Americans who were interned and who eventually returned to Japan after the war.

Yoshiko Uchida, Desert Exile. Seattle: University of Washington Press, 1982. The author's account of her life as a young internee in Topaz Relocation Center.

Michi Weglyn, Years of Infamy. New York: William Morrow, Quill Paperbacks, 1976. The story of Japanese American internment, including details on conditions at Tule Lake Segregation Center and attorney Wayne Collins's fight to restore the citizenship of those who renounced in 1944.

Internet Sources

"Chinese Exclusion Act," 47th Cong., sess. 1, 1882. www.itp.berkeley.edu/~asam121/1882.html. Text of the 1882 exclusion act that barred Chinese immigration into the United States for ten years.

Ex Parte Mitsuye Endo, December 18, 1944. http://history.wisc.edu/archdeacon/404tja/endo.html. The Supreme Court ruling that brought an end to internment.

Henry C. Pratt, Public Proclamation No. 21, Western Defense Command, U.S. Army, December 17, 1944. www.du.edu/~amballar/PP_21.html. The official announcement ending exclusion of Japanese Americans from the Pacific Coast.

Franklin Delano Roosevelt, "The Four Freedoms," January 6, 1941. www.libertynet.org/~edcivic/fdr.html. Text of President Franklin Roosevelt's speech delivered to Congress just months before the United States entered World War II.

Index

Picture Credits

About the Author

Diane Yancy worked as a freelance writer in the Pacific Northwest, where she has lived for over twenty years. She writes nonfiction for middle-grade and high-school, readers, and enjoys traveling and collecting old books. Some of her other titles include *Civil War Generals of the Union*, *Leaders of the Civil War*, and *Strategic Battles of the Civil War*.